MEMOIRS

OF
EARL MACPHERSON
THE KING OF "PIN-UP ART"

By EARL MACPHERSON and
MERYLENE SCHNEIDER

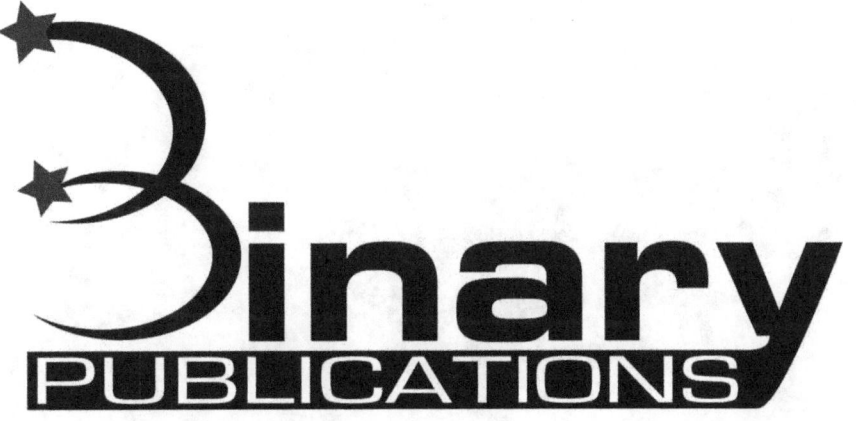

To Reathel and Michael and
all those lovely girls who graced my canvases–and
to Paul Burke who thought my autobiography
reads like "A DAMN MOVIE!"

mac Pherson

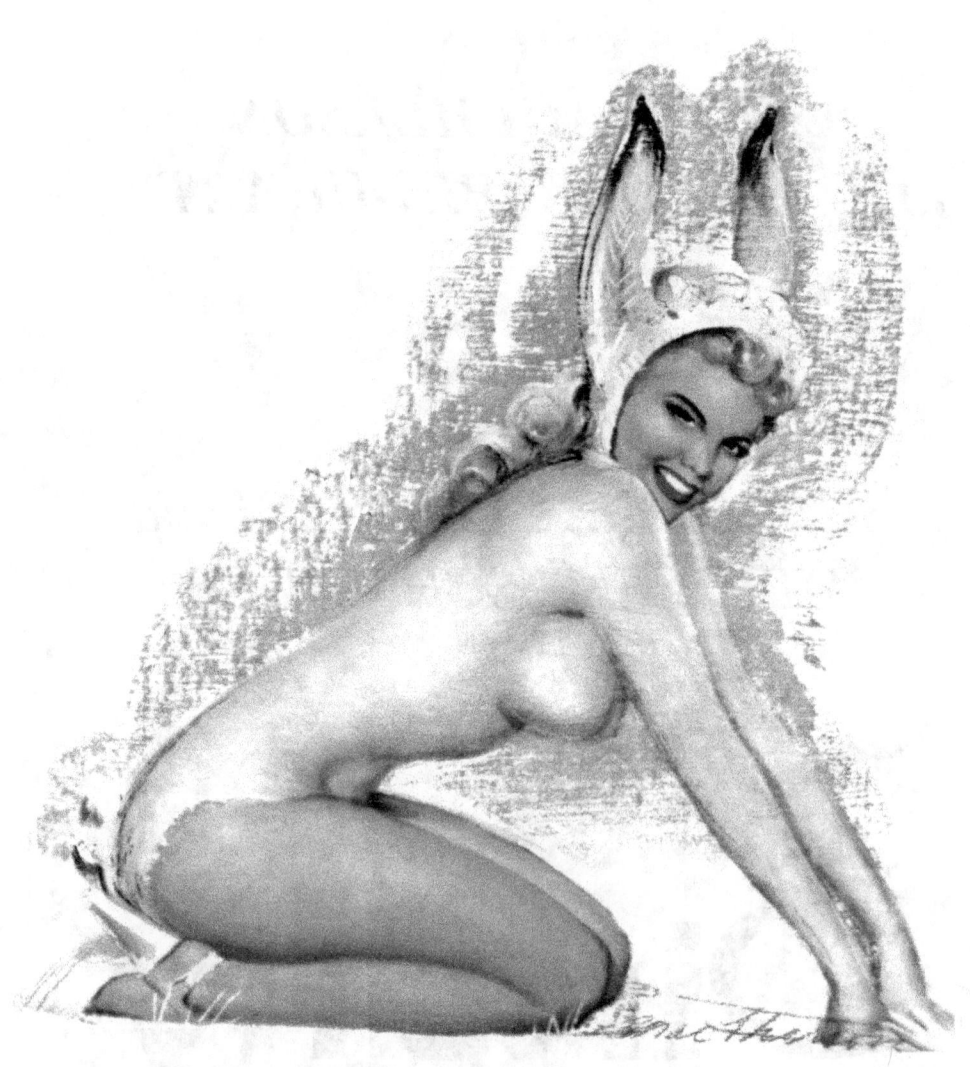

MEMOIRS
OF EARL MACPHERSON
THE KING OF "PIN-UP ART!"

By EARL MACPHERSON and
MERYLENE SCHNEIDER

Cover artwork "MEMOIRS" from the collection of
Mr. and Mrs. Al Grasmoen.
Page 8 artwork "Herbert Hoover III" from the collection of
Mr. and Mrs. Herbert Hoover II.

Printed in the United States of America

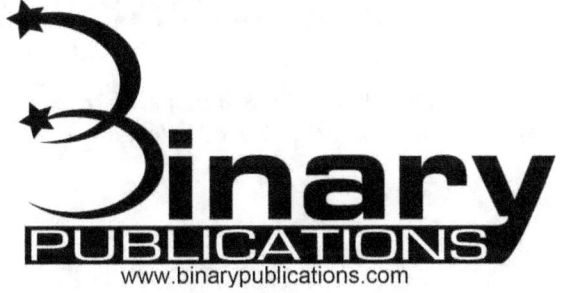

www.binarypublications.com

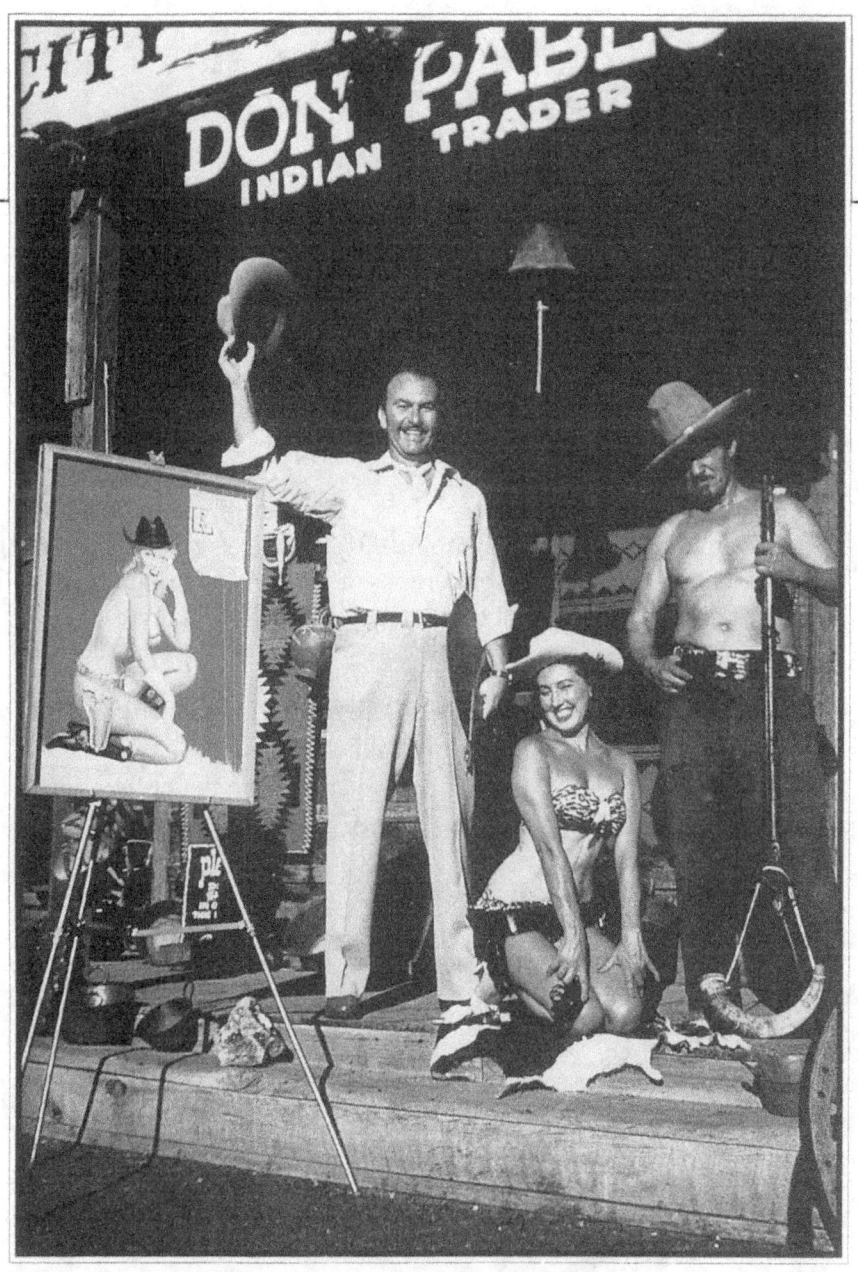

"How The West Was Won!" Scottsdale, Arizona, 1954.
"Mac" (the Artist), "Maxie" (the Model), and Pablo.

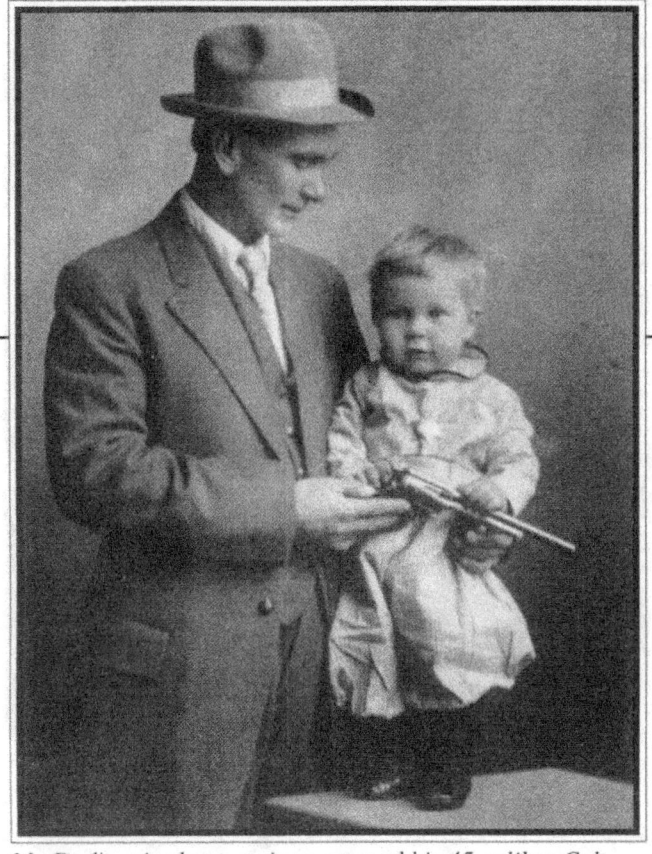

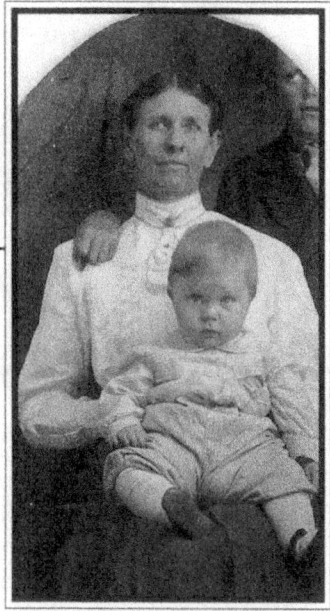

*My first photo, on my Grand-
mother Sarah's lap, 1911.*

*My Dad's prized possessions: me and his 45 caliber Colt,
c. 1913.*

Artist Earl MacPherson was born in a small, white frame house on his grandfather's farm in Oklahoma, on August 3, 1910. His father, William David MacPherson, was short of cash, so he paid the country doctor with a live pig.

"As soon as I could see, Dad began giving me art lessons, " says Earl. "Not that he was much of an artist."

"Old Bill," as his father was called, had been a professional hunter in the early days of Oklahoma until his son came along. To make a better life for their family, Earl's mother, who was born Ida Elvira Love, made her husband quit hunting, which he loved, and start farming, which he hated. As a result, "Old Bill" took up drinking and chasing women.

When Earl was only six years old, he started following his father from one saloon to another watching him draw pictures for drinks. Earl soon began to imitate his dad, making sketches of guns, Stetson hats, horses and naked women for a sarsaparilla. Since Earl was having some difficulty doing the pictures of naked women, his father tried to sneak him into a willing lady's house in nearby Crescent, Oklahoma, for some firsthand life study.

"Mom caught us and was so irate that I gave up nudes until I was in art school," recalls Earl.

However, Earl continued on with his artwork, trading sketches for the other kid's lunches at school, and winning a blue ribbon at the county fair.

"Dad attempted to get art on the school's curriculum, but since I was the only artist in the entire school, he failed, " says Earl. "So it was that my family, like a lot of other Okies, migrated to California, in search of the good life and an art teacher for me."

The Mac Phersons settled in the small city of Redlands, nestled in the foothills of the Sierra Madre mountains, about sixty miles east of Los Angeles. Both his mother and father went to work at a fruit packing house that specialized in sun-ripened oranges. Earl went to school.

Finally, when he reached high school, there were art classes available, and an eager, inspirational teacher, Mary Louise Arnold. Miss Arnold was an excellent tutor, able to bring out and develop the talents of her most serious students, many of whom went on to become renowned artists. For example, one of Walt Disney's first animators, Preston Blair, was her pupil.

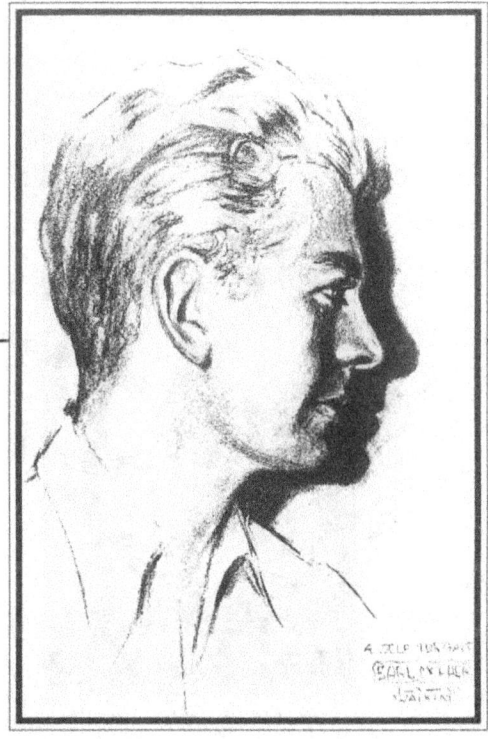

Self–portrait, Hawaii, 1931.

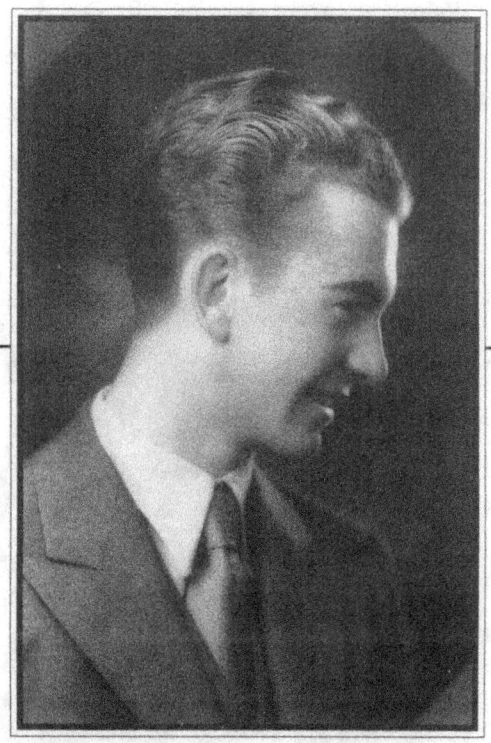

Graduation photo, 1928.

Earl's art teacher had the habit of pairing the best boy students with the best girl students and sending them off to the nearby mountains or desert together to sketch or paint. Earl comments:

"I made great strides at Redlands High, and graduated as president of the class of '28. I also 'made' straight A's in Art, a drama major and a student teacher."

Summers were spent working on his uncle's H-V Ranch in Springerville, Arizona, helping the cook gather wood, washing dishes and occasionally riding a gentle cow-pony. After seeing some of Earl's sketches, his aunt insisted that he not do any rough work that might damage his hands. This experience on the ranch was giving Earl material that he would use later in life when he began to do "Western Art."

After high school, Earl enrolled at the San Bernardino Valley Union Junior College, but soon decided that their art classes were lusterless. At mid-term, he moved to Los Angeles, where he found a job days making movie posters for a downtown theater.

Evenings, Earl enrolled in a life drawing class, taught by figure painter Lawrence Murphey at the new Chouinard School of Art. This was Earl's first proper instruction at sketching the nude figure. He says that Murphey soon taught him to look upon the nude female figure as something more than a naked girl. He learned body proportions, where the bones are, and how to delineate form with charcoal.

"I also learned that if you want to find out how to paint the nude female form you must first learn to leave the nude female models alone," he adds.

Unable to form any close relations with the models, Earl started to spend his weekends back in Redlands with the student teacher he had been involved with during his senior year of high school. She loved the record "Honey," whose flip side, "Song of the Islands," they would play part of the time.

This Hawaiian melody must have had an effect on Earl, for when he discovered the honey blonde student teacher in a compromising position with her English professor, Earl cashed in his life savings and bought passage on the first ship to Honolulu.

Enroute to Hawaii, Earl picked up spending money by sketching the passengers for five dollars per head. One of his customers was Hayward B. Delavan, who had left his wife in Ventura to seek adventure in the South Seas. Within a week of landing, Del and Earl had built a grass shack on the sea wall overlooking Waikiki Beach. Del liked their spot on the wall so much that he bought it. Earl found a job at a bookstore in downtown Honolulu, doing quick sketches for five dollars apiece, but Del soon persuaded him to give it up and try to find an agent.

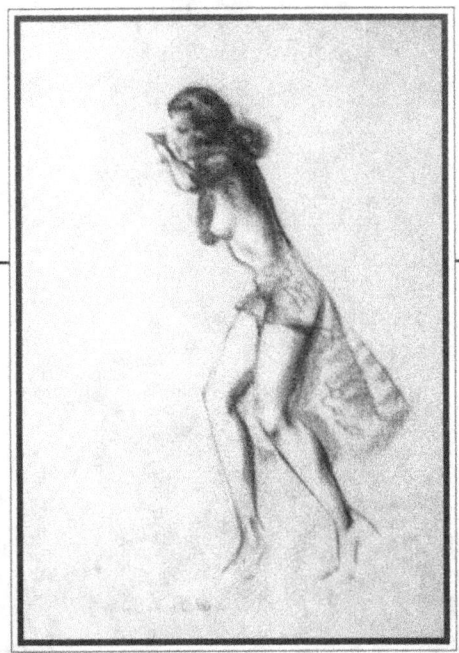

Rhoda Fulton, my first pin–up model, c. 1936.

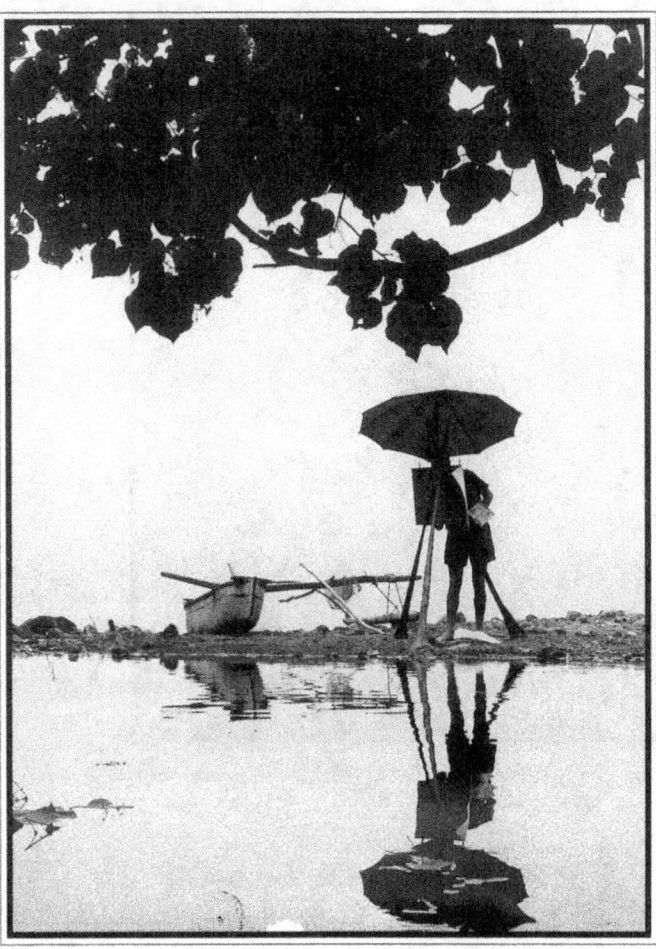

Painting on Kauai, c. 1938.

Luckily, Richard Post was opening a new art gallery in the lobby of the Royal Hawaiian Hotel and was looking for an artist to do charcoal portraits of the hotel clientele. Earl's price was raised from $5 to $50 per commission, which he had to split fifty-fifty with Post, who was acting as his agent. (Before Earl left Hawaii, his price had doubled.)

When Earl received his first earnings, he tried to share them with Del, who had encouraged him and helped him find the position. Del refused, insisting that they were living in their little shack rent-free. Earl tells what happened next:

"After Del told me that I owed him nothing, he commented that he did need someone with whom to play tennis every morning. Naturally, I offered my services. Del suggested that whoever won should do the dishes each day. Knowing I was a lot younger, I added, 'Let's include all the housework.' For the next year, Del lived a life of luxury, waited on by a six-foot blond artist —me!"

The next summer, Del and Earl added another room onto their shack, and Del's seventeen-year-old niece, Trudy, and a family friend, Miss Spaulding, came to visit them from California. Earl spent most of his time entertaining the niece and showing her Hawaii, totally neglecting his art. After a harrowing experience on a remote beach, with Earl having to rescue Trudy from the ocean's undertow and getting caught in it himself for a while, the two of them decided that they would spend the rest of their lives together.

That September, Trudy and Miss Spaulding returned to California so that Trudy could begin attending college. The next month, Del, who was getting restless, sold his Waikiki Beach frontage and booked passage for Tahiti. When Del left in November, Earl went back Stateside to find Trudy, determined to renew his career in art and make a success of it for her sake.

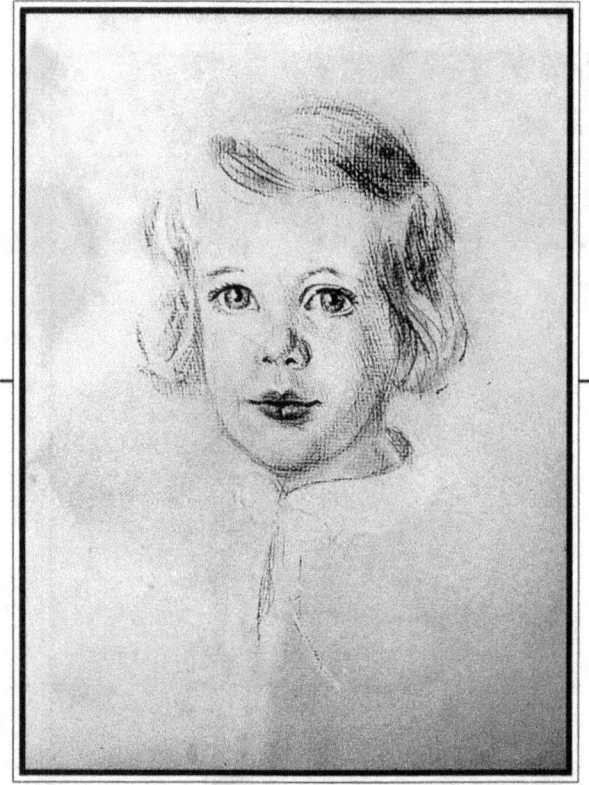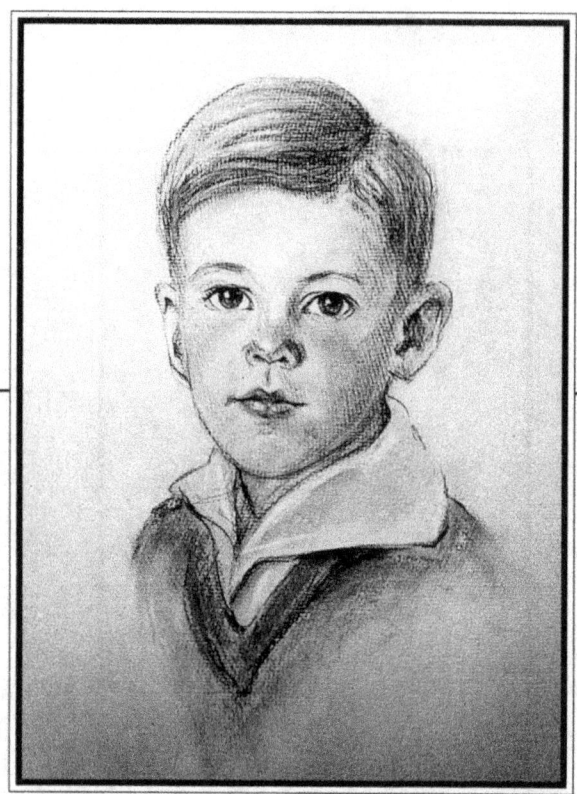

Two of the portraits of President Herbert Hoover's grandchildren that I did in 1931.

Docking in San Francisco, Earl immediately phoned Trudy's home in Ventura, only to discover that she was in Los Angeles attending UCLA. Unable to reach her, Earl went home to Redlands, where he found a position doing charcoal sketches at the Harris Department Store. To celebrate his son's homecoming, "Old Bill" bought a new 1930 Ford convertible, and lent it to Earl during Christmas vacation so he could go visit Trudy.

"Trudy's family warmly welcomed me, pleased with the portrait I gave them that I had made of Trudy when we were in Hawaii. However, her mother soon distanced herself from me when she discovered that I could only earn twenty-five dollars for such paintings in California, although I was receiving one hundred dollars for them just before I left the Islands," says Earl.

After Christmas, Earl sailed to San Francisco by freighter and obtained jobs at two department stores doing portraits. He hoped to earn enough money so that he could marry Trudy. He also enrolled in art classes at the San Francisco School of Fine Arts.

"I guess Trudy was persuaded to view me through her mother's critical eyes; I was never able to reach Trudy at school that next semester, and when I went to see her the next summer, I discovered that she had gone to Europe with her mother. I never saw her again."

Deciding to spread his wings, and trying to forget Trudy, the following autumn Earl began holding exhibits at some of the fashionable resorts and hotels in California. On this social circuit, Earl was again receiving $100 per portrait, especially when the pictures were framed and offered in the right gallery. Also, he was beginning to obtain commissions to do portraits, including one of the lovely movie actress, Katherine MacDonald.

In November of 1931, while exhibiting in Pasadena, Earl received his greatest commission, that of painting President Herbert Hoover's grandchildren. For one week, Earl practically lived with the Herbert Hoover, Jr., family while he did pastels of their three well-behaved children. As word spread that he was the artist who had done the President's grandchildren, Earl was deluged with commissions for work for the coming year.

The next Christmas, Earl went home to Redlands in triumph. The Harrises (owners of the department store) threw a cocktail party in his honor and invited his first art teacher, Mary Louise Arnold.

"Miss Arnold advised me not to get carried away with my success. She also urged me to find someone who could teach me to paint in oils," says Earl.

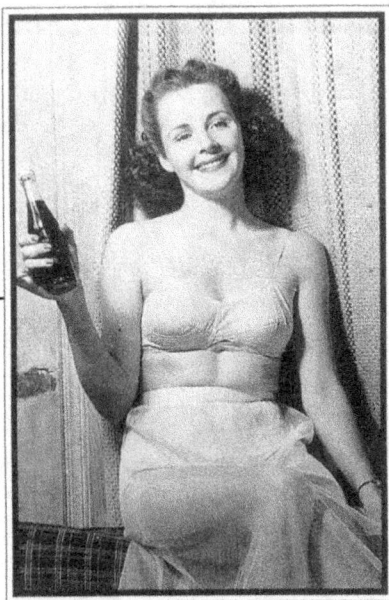

Coca–Cola ad model, 1939

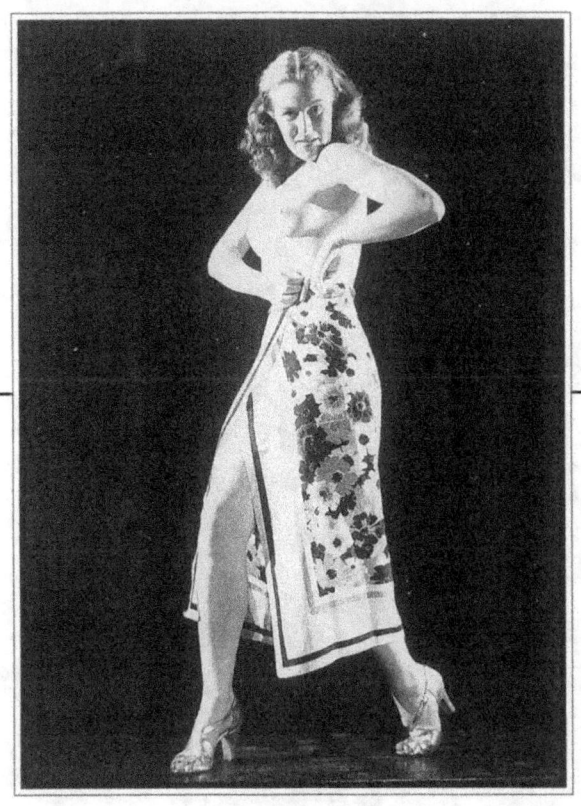

Camera class model, 1938

"Because there was considerable wealth in Redlands, and the possibility of more commissions, I decided to remain there for the rest of the winter. I rented a room in an old three-story mansion and turned it into a studio. I rediscovered a beautiful young Chicano, Bonnie Hill, who was willing to be my model. Bonnie had been a freshman when I was a senior at Redlands High. At twenty-two years of age, I thought I had it made."

One day, Earl received an invitation to speak at San Bernardino Junior College. Afterwards, one of the students came forward and introduced herself. Her name was Dianne Miller. By summer, Earl and Dianne were married. They rented a small, brown cottage in the pretty little seacoast town of La Jolla, while Earl exhibited his artwork and did portraits in the sprawling Casa de Mañana Hotel close by. A beautiful, and very sexy-looking, young woman, Dianne often posed for her new husband to sketch her.

It was at the hotel that Earl met an English bartender named Tommy Morgan. When business was slow, Tommy taught Earl how to "drain" the slot machines that had been put in the Casa de Mañana by some enterprising gangsters. After they had a little too much to drink, Tommy would persuade his wealthy customers to play the machines. Later, before the gangsters came to empty them, Earl would extract the profits using Tommy's "technique," while Tommy acted as look-out. Then the two of them shared the money.

This cash enabled the newlyweds to get by, for opportunities in the portrait business were starting to be scarce. Earl had thought it was due to the depression, but in time realized that there was another factor:

"I discovered that the portrait business for artists was coming to a standstill because of a development that I could not have anticipated: color photography. It had become fashionable to have one's portrait done in this medium, rather than being painted. La Jolla now had two or three excellent photographers and they had already learned to glamorize their subjects. Since it was less expensive and the results were good, eventually color photography almost completely replaced the artist's portrait on the American scene."

Meanwhile, Tommy invented a gadget for mixing drinks and earned enough money from it to open his own gambling establishment. He gave Earl a studio upstairs to use rent-free, and ten percent of the gambling profits, in exchange for bringing customers to the game rooms. Tommy encouraged Earl to paint nudes, hanging them over the bar, and showing them off to the visiting gamblers.

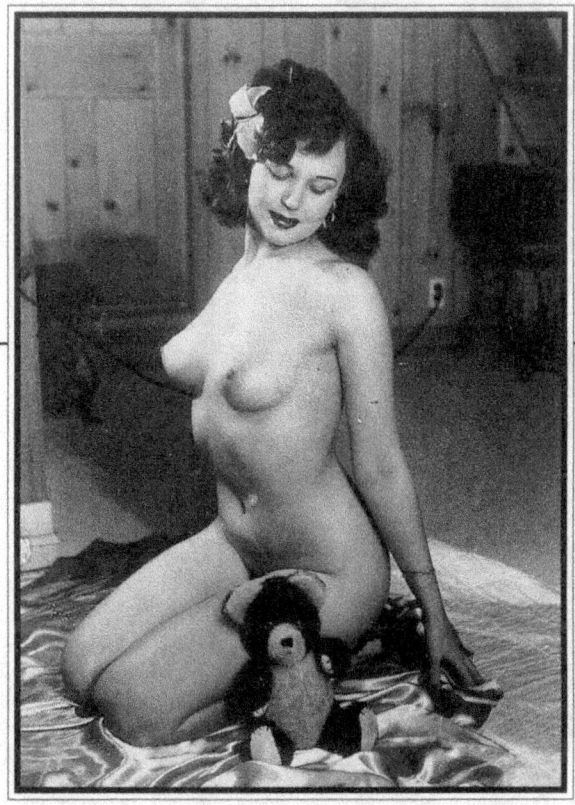

Betty Morelius, a Minneapolis beauty, 1940

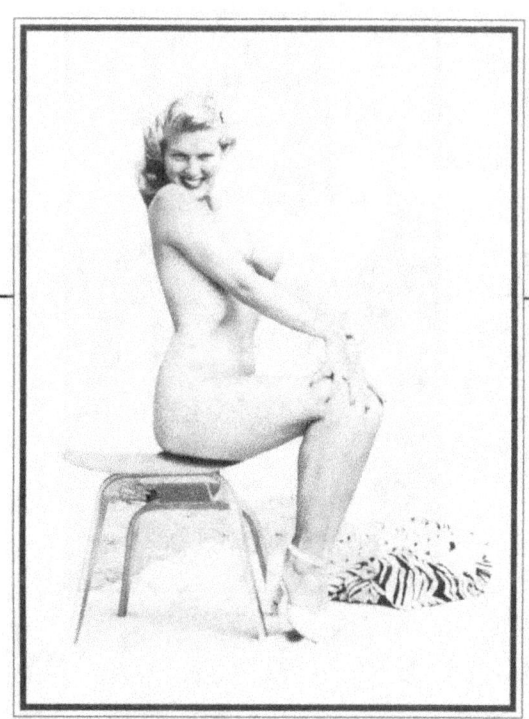

"Fun–Hunting" model, Minta Hoia D'roney.

When Dianne found out how Earl was earning his living, she objected, especially after the place was raided. Earl was released because he had no previous record, but the judge had to be convinced of Tommy's innocence. Afterwards, Earl and Tommy closed up their respective businesses, and the newlyweds left town.

The next few years were difficult ones, with Dianne following Earl to Phoenix, Colorado Springs, and finally back to La Jolla, as he tried to earn a living with art exhibits and the faltering business of portrait painting. The situation was not eased with the birth of a son, Michael. Dianne's sister, Mary Lee, moved in with them. Soon after that, Dianne and Earl had a daughter, Sylvia. Mary Lee often bought groceries and helped her sister with the babies.

One summer, when Earl was exhibiting at Lake Arrowhead, he did the family portraits of an older, attractive socialite, on vacation from Beverly Hills. Because her husband was busy having an affair with his French secretary, the socialite, Lorraine, cast her eyes on Earl. She talked many of her friends into having their portraits done by him, and ultimately persuaded Earl to follow her back to Beverly Hills. Here, as luck would have it, he ran into his English pal, Tommy.

Tommy was bartending again, at the famed Cock and Bull restaurant on Sunset Strip in Hollywood. At the time, "the Strip" was one of the most glamorous streets in the world. Top Hollywood agents had their offices there and the smartest night clubs and shops lined both sides of the street. Rent was high, but there happened to be an empty store in the building across from the Cock and Bull, and Tommy had another plan. He told Earl that they were going to open a new art gallery in the space.

"I said to him, 'I'd love it, Tommy...but I'm broke.'

"'Never mind that,' he replied, in his best cockney accent. 'Just get all your paintings together, including some nudes. I'll take care of the rest.'

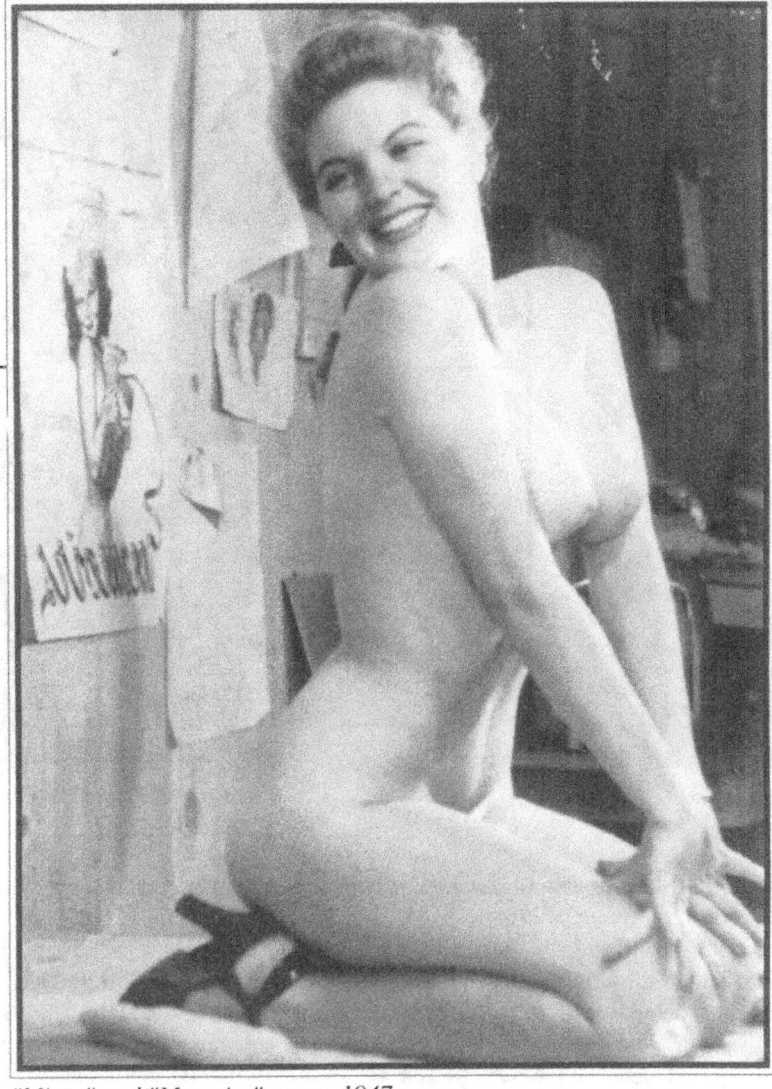

"Minta" and "Memoirs" cover, 1947.

"By the time the smoke cleared, we had opened Hollywood's first 'Art Gallery and Booking Establishment'. My exhibits were up front, along with some paintings by Harry Waggoner of Palm Springs and the great English painter Gordon Couts. In the back, behind a fancy partition, Tommy and his pals were running a bookmaking operation on the horses."

Things went well for them from the beginning. The gallery was frequented by many celebrities, such as Nelson Eddy and Frank Morgan. Earl did a portrait of the beautiful English actress, Verree Teasdale, and a sketch of Deanna Durbin for a movie magazine. He also continued to do nudes, examples of which Tommy would hang behind the bar at the restaurant. Most importantly, Earl was now able to send money home to Dianne and the children.

Afternoons, after the horse racing was over for the day, Earl closed the gallery and went joyriding with Lorraine in her powder blue Cadillac. Sometimes he'd wander across the street to the Cock and Bull, where Tommy would give him dart lessons. Eventually, the lessons paid off. Tommy would get his best customers high on Pimm's Cups, then con them into a dart game with "that famous artist from across the street." Earl would put up a nude painting against fifty dollars and the game would begin.

"We usually let the customer win the first game, and then raised the stakes. With my accurate eye and the sensitive touch of an artist, my opponents usually didn't have a chance. And, of course, if one of them seemed to be winning too much, despite the odds, Tommy could simply load his drink with a touch of Mickey Finn."

One such situation resulted in Earl and Tommy winning a new La Salle cabriolet from David Niven's brother. It was a very exciting, down-to-the-wire match between two excellent dart players, one a fine young Englishman, who had enjoyed too many Pimm's Cups, and the other, Earl, who was drinking mostly Coca-Cola.

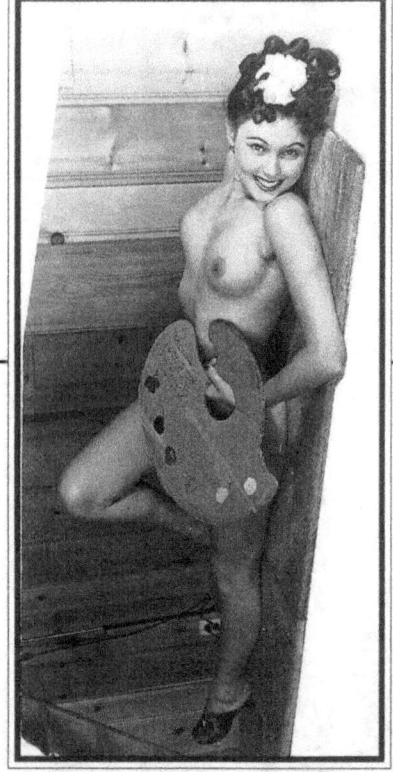

Betty.

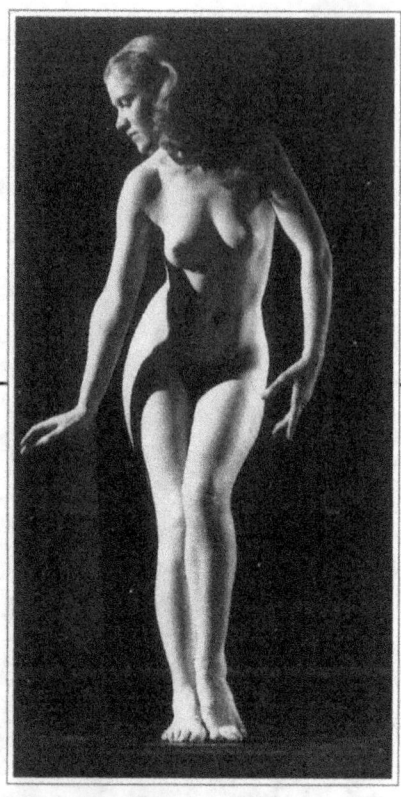

Earl Carroll model, 1938.

"Tommy and I took turns using our new La Salle. He would drive it to work one week and I, the next. In between times, I could borrow Lorraine's Cadillac, so I traveled in style."

In regards to style, Lorraine had decided to make a gentleman out of Earl, so she set about teaching him better table manners and trying to refine his speech, which still held elements of his Oklahoma background. She introduced Earl to all her friends in her Beverly Hills' social set, and hired detectives to follow her husband, millionaire Chester Herrick of the brokerage firm of Haskell and Herrick, so she could file for divorce. Finally, she outfitted Earl in an elegant new wardrobe.

"Tommy hardly recognized me when I showed up at the Cock and Bull in Bond Street clothes. He bought me a drink and kept surveying me proudly.

"'You're going up in the world, Earl,' he said in his cockney tone, 'You're even beginning to act like a gentleman. Oh, by the way, there was a man in here looking for you. He wants you to come on over to the Earl Carroll Theater.'"

Earl Carroll's theater was the showplace of Hollywood and the Earl Carroll Girls who performed there were beautiful. The manager wanted Earl Mac Pherson to paint some of the girls for posters in the theater lobby. They came down to Earl's studio to pose in their showgirl costumes, which, as Earl remembers, "were close to nothing at all."

All at once, the "Art Gallery and Booking Establishment" became the most popular spot on the Strip. Wealthy bachelors and agents crowded the studio, until there was hardly room for Earl to paint. Even the bookies in the back room stopped taking bets and came forward to watch the girls posing. Earl comments:

"However, the fellows that gave me the most trouble were the B & B Boys, salesmen from Brown & Bigelow, the world's largest calendar company, situated in St. Paul, Minnesota. These salesmen kept trying to tell me how to pose the Carroll beauties. In fact, they even brought their manager in to see me painting the girls, and then, within a day or two, they returned with one of the B & B vice-presidents, Frank Van Keuren."

Van Keuren told Earl, "Mac Pherson, I think you should be painting calendars for us."

"I'm doing pretty good here. What do you pay for calendar art– fifty dollars a sketch?" Earl asked.

The salesmen snickered, as Van Keuren casually answered, "Oh, my no! B & B buys only the best paintings in the world for our calendars. We pay our pin-up artists a thousand dollars apiece for their pictures."

Earl was definitely interested. "When I realized that Van Keuren was serious, I put down my pastels and looked over at the salesmen for confirmation. They nodded in agreement with their boss. They were as serious as men can be, with a practically nude showgirl smiling at them. I turned to B & B's vice-president and said, "'Mr. Van Keuren, I think you've got a deal.'"

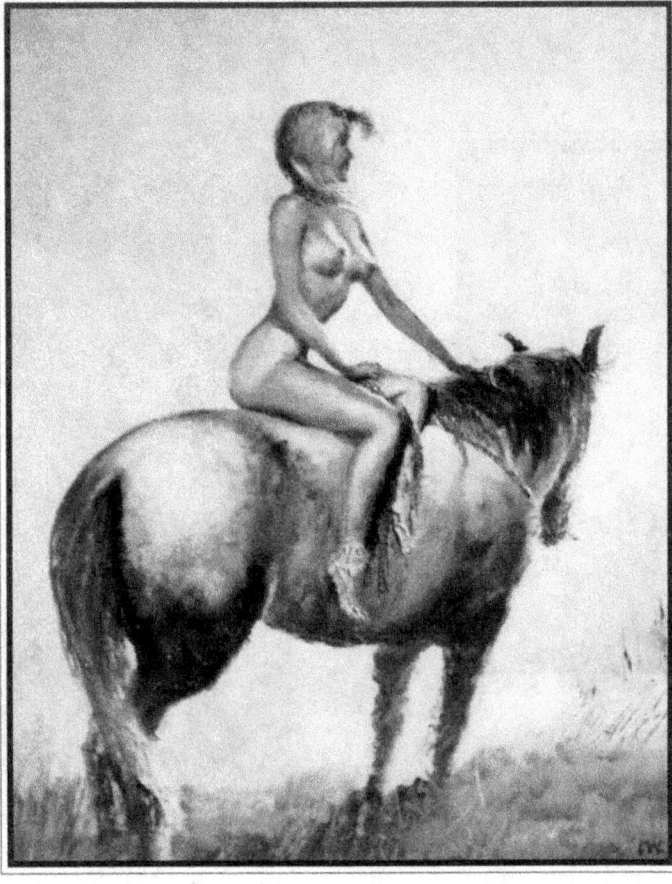

My first "Lady Godiva," from the collection of Max Allen Collins.

Over lunch, Van Keuren informed Earl that the only thing left to be done was to persuade Charles Ward, the president of Brown & Bigelow, of Earl's talent and value to the calendar industry. Van Keuren said that Ward had final say on the hiring of all his artists.

Ward was going to be in the Los Angeles area the next week on his honeymoon and might be willing to see Earl.

Van Keuren wanted Earl to paint a large picture of a nude for Charles Ward to see. On the advice of the B & B salesmen and their district manager, Earl decided to paint a life-size picture of Lady Godiva, done with patriotic touches of red, white and blue. Then he convinced one of the Carroll girls to pose for it.

Before beginning the actual painting, Earl contacted his good friend Bob Adams, who worked in the art department for Western Lithographic, and showed him the preliminary sketches. Adams was asked for any suggestions.

"To begin with, most girl calendars are vertical hangers and the sketch that you've made is a horizontal composition, so see if you can change that," Adams said. "And forget about the horse. Calendar buyers are mostly all men, and they prefer two-legged nudes to four-legged ones."

Adams told Earl that this opportunity was a once-in-a-lifetime deal.

"Mac," he said, "if you pull this off, you'll be the envy of every illustrator in the country. If Charlie Ward hires you, you'll be starting at the very top of the profession."

Adams raised objections when Earl told him that he would be meeting Ward when he came to California on his honeymoon:

"Ward's not going to want to be bothered with an artist when he's on his honeymoon. He will have better things to do," said Adams. "But I do know that he is going to take a few minutes to tend to business. He will be coming down here to Western Litho, 'cause he's thinking of buying the company. You get your picture done and let me take care of the rest."

Earl had heard that before from Tommy, and it had resulted in their successful gallery and booking house, so he went back to the studio and set to work. Using his lovely model, he painted the biggest and best nude picture he had ever done: Lady Godiva stood against a sky blue background, almost six feet high, with a red ribbon in her hair. The paint was still wet when Bob Adams phoned Earl and said for him to bring the painting down to Western Litho early the next morning as Ward was due there at 9:30 a.m.

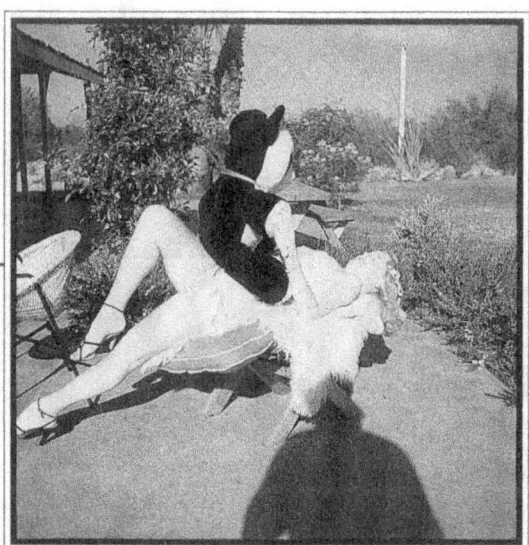

"Barely Yours," 1950.

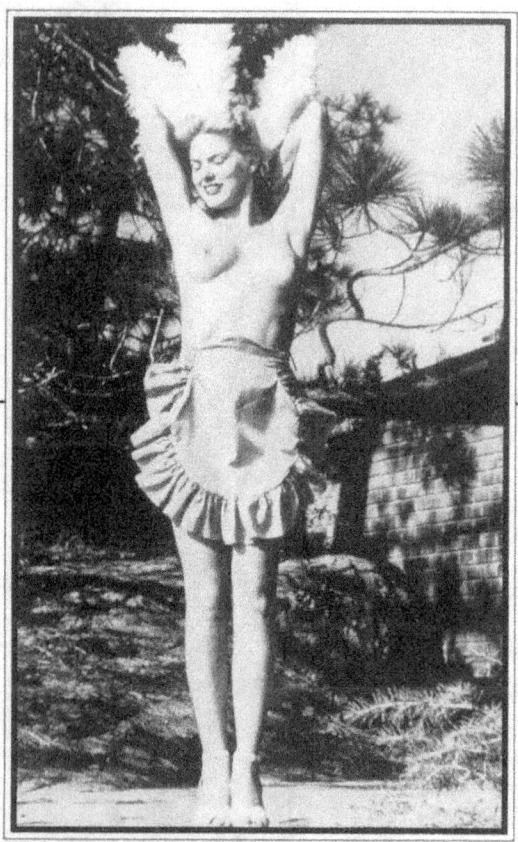

Minta Hoia at "Cliffhaven,"
my John Lloyd Wright-designed studio, 1950.

"How am I going to get the painting all the way to downtown Los Angeles?" Earl asked. "It's six feet high!"

"Why the hell did you make it so big?" demanded Adams.

"The B & B Boys told me to."

"That's just like salesmen. Well, don't worry, I'll send a truck out for you and Lady Godiva early tomorrow."

When Earl and his masterpiece arrived at Western Litho, Adams showed him into a small office and said, "Ward is due to be in the next office in a few minutes. Just listen to me and follow my lead."

As soon as they heard voices through the thin wall partition, Adams spoke up in his loudest voice:

"Mister Mac Pherson, this is without a doubt the best damn girl subject I have ever seen! Unquestionably, Lady Godiva is going to make calendar history. How much do you want for the painting?"

"One thousand dollars, Mr. Adams, " Earl replied.

Adams continued shouting in the direction of the wall, "Not bad...not bad, at all. I'm not sure Western Litho can pay you that much, but the Murphy Calendar Company is trying to muscle into the big time. I believe they would buy it, so if we don't, I'll contact them for you."

Immediately, the voices in the next room grew louder,

"What do I do now?" whispered Earl.

"Take your painting and get back to your studio in Hollywood as fast as you can," replied Adams.

The phone was ringing by the time Earl and his "Lady" had reached the art gallery; it was the district manager for Brown & Bigelow:

"Mac, what the hell's the idea of trying to sell your picture to our competitors?"

"I was showing her to an old friend," Earl protested innocently.

"Now you listen, Mac, and listen good! Ward was there in the next room and heard you. He damn well doesn't want anybody else to have any really good pin-up artists. He's here in our office now, but he wants you to meet him at the Bridal Suite at the Beverly Wilshire Hotel, as soon as possible. I'll come out and get you and we'll go down there together. Be sure and bring the painting," said the manager.

"Okay, I will, but only if you can bring a truck to haul it."

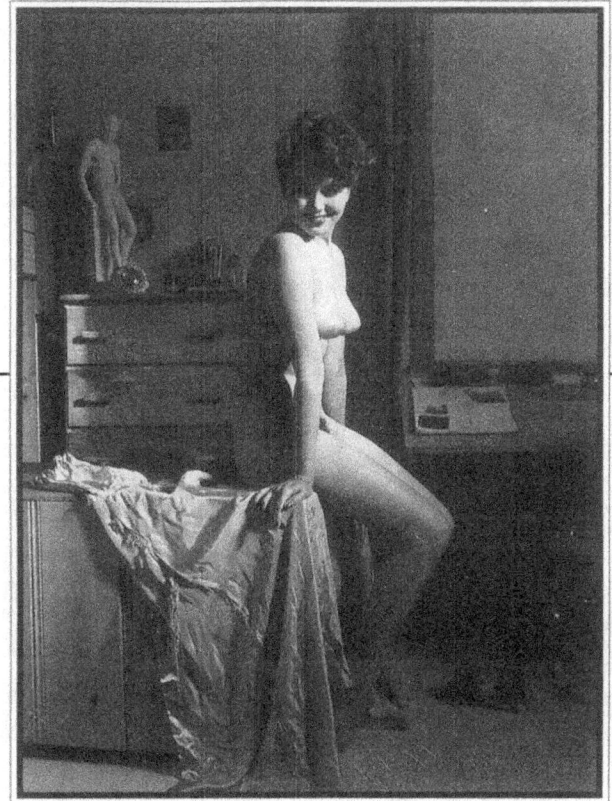

"Betty" poses in my Minneapolis studio, 1940, for the first "Artist's Sketchpad."

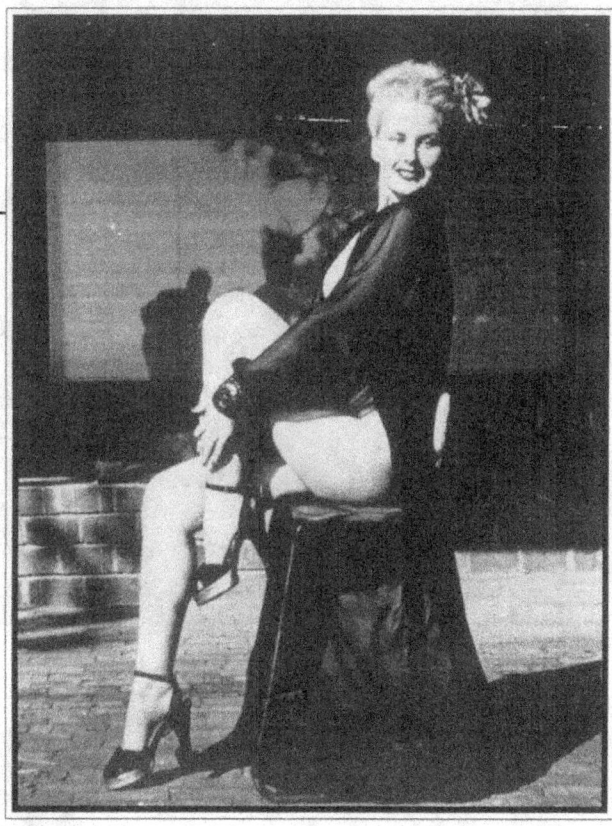

Jean Lofthouse, a gorgeous blonde model, Del Mar, California, 1952.

The naked Lady Godiva almost caused a riot as the two men carried the huge painting through the hotel lobby. Upstairs, Earl was ushered in to meet Charles Allen Ward by his lovely bride, Yvette. Ward was a powerfully-built, middle-aged man with his head shaved clean as a billiard ball.

"He had quite a presence. His eyes seemed to bore right through me," Earl remembers. "He surveyed Lady Godiva briefly and asked: 'What's this about you trying to sell your painting to another calendar company? Don't ever do that again!'

"Then he turned to his subordinate and ordered, 'Put Mac Pherson, or whatever his name is, on the payroll, immediately, then get him on the train back to St. Paul as soon as he can pack.'

"'Yes, sir, Mr. Ward. How about his painting?' asked the district manager.

"'Oh, Hell! Crate it and ship it back to Minnesota, too,' said the great man.

"My interview was completed in less than five minutes, leaving me with a job at the largest calendar company in the world."

Tommy and Lorraine were delighted with Earl's good news. Tommy agreed to buy out Earl's share of the "Art Gallery and Booking Establishment." Lorraine said that she would have her lawyer help Earl to get a divorce from Dianne. (A divorce that was never contested.) Lorraine planned on marrying Earl when he returned from making his fortune in St. Paul, even though he was closer in age to her nineteen-year-old son, than to her.

The next morning, Earl boarded the Santa Fe for his trip to Minnesota, stopping in San Bernardino to see his mother and father, before continuing on his way. As the train traveled north, Earl recalled that it was "Old Bill" who had first started him off on his "Adventures in Art."

Earl was met at the station by Frank Van Keuren, who had returned home the day before. Frank and his wife graciously opened their home to Earl and offered him living quarters in their spacious house near the beginnings of the Mississippi River.

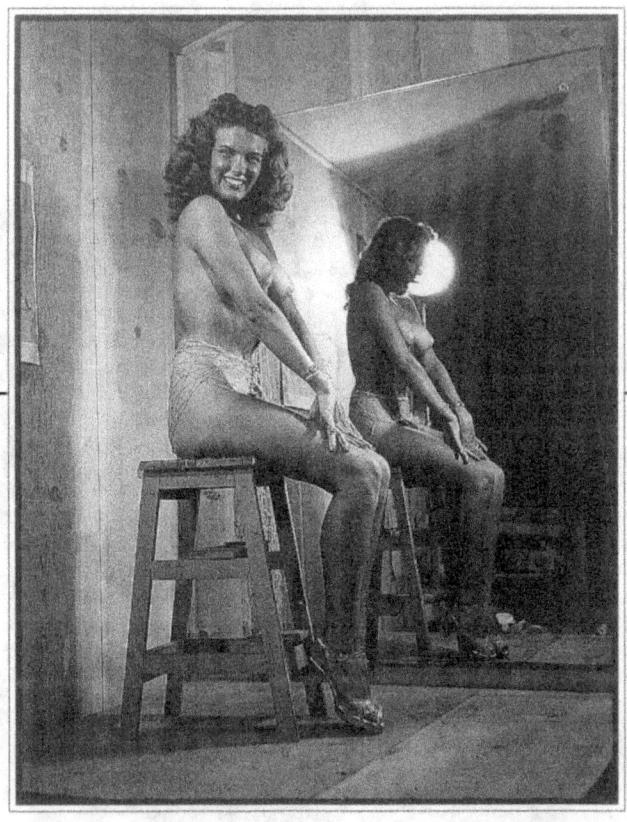

Minta learns to pose, 1945.

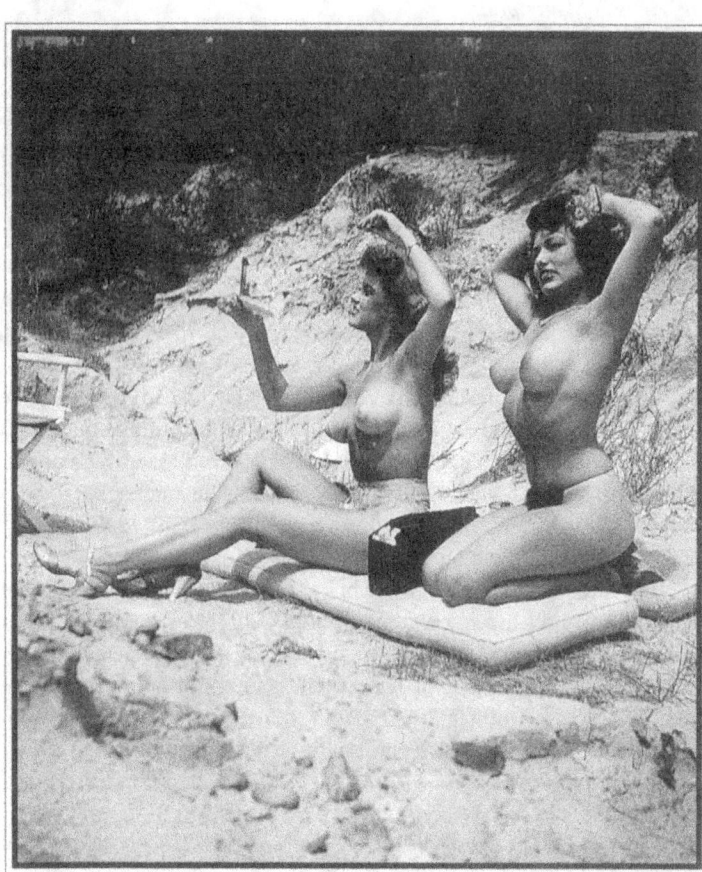

Enter Lili, Hispanic beauty, with Minta, 1947.

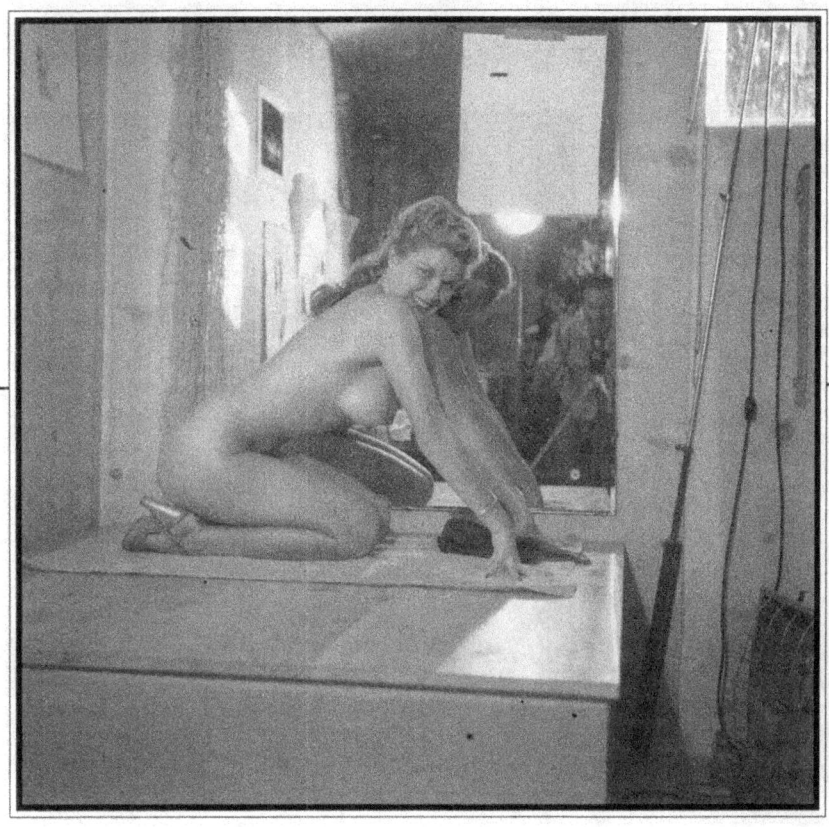

Minta poses for rabbit sketch, 1947.

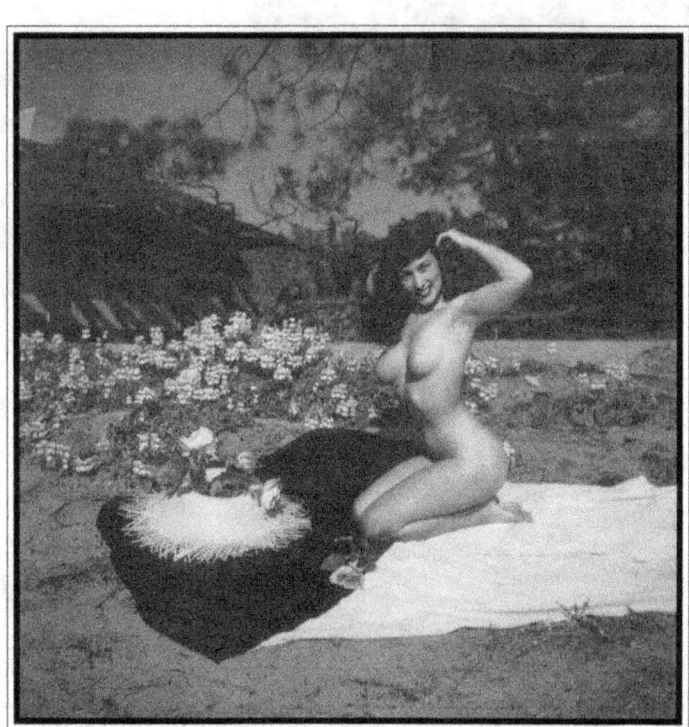

Lili, in front of Del Mar studio, 1952.

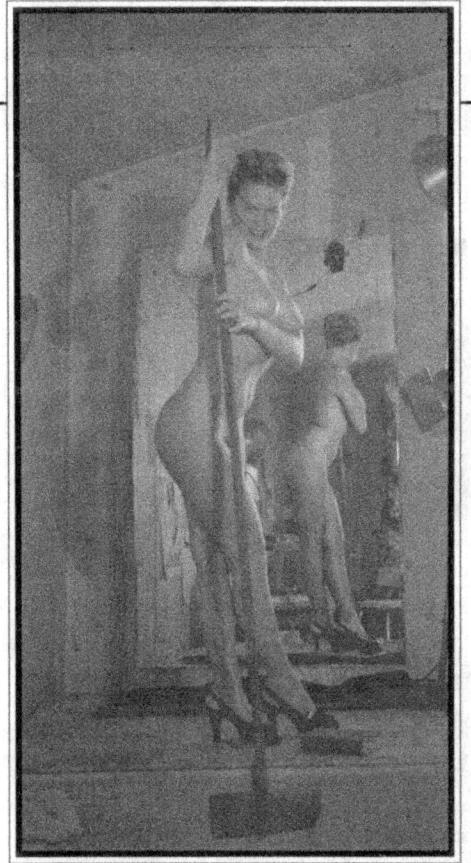

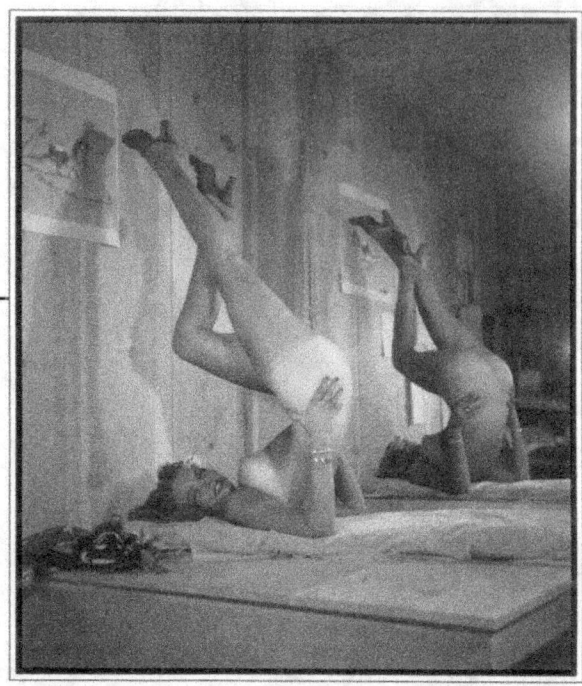

More pin-up poses and a Scottsdale beauty, 1954.

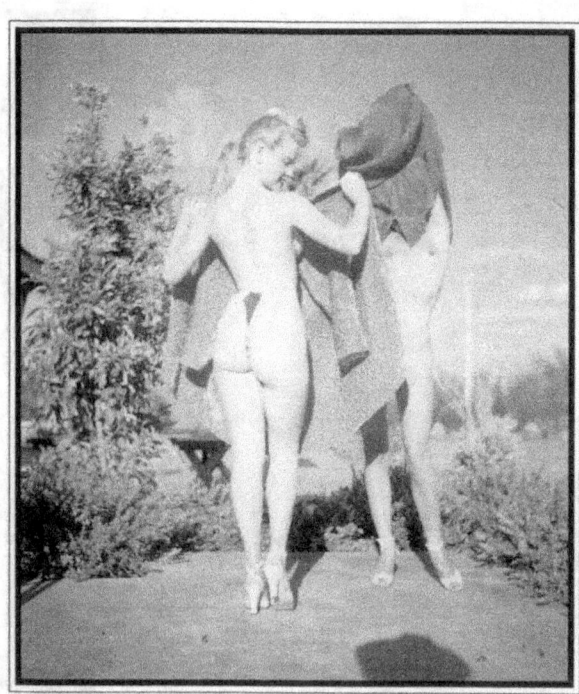

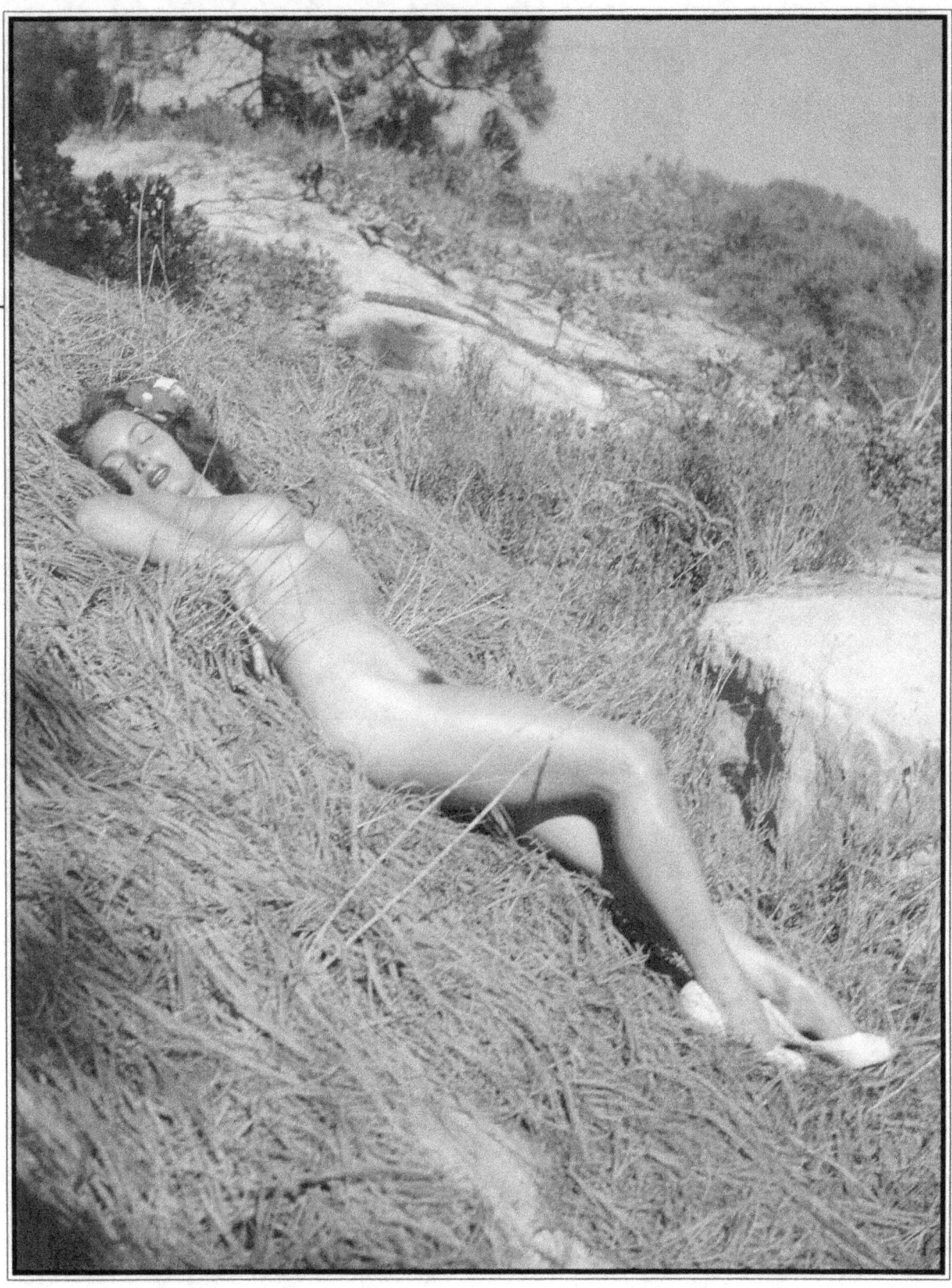

Lili in one of my finest photos, taken in a forest of Torrey pines, near Del Mar, California, 1953.

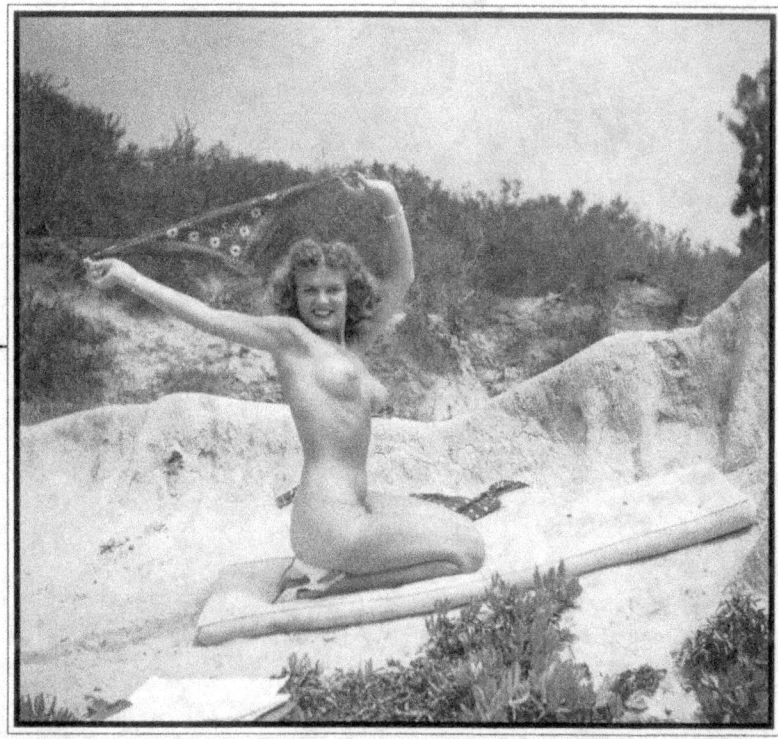

Minta, on sand dunes, 1946.

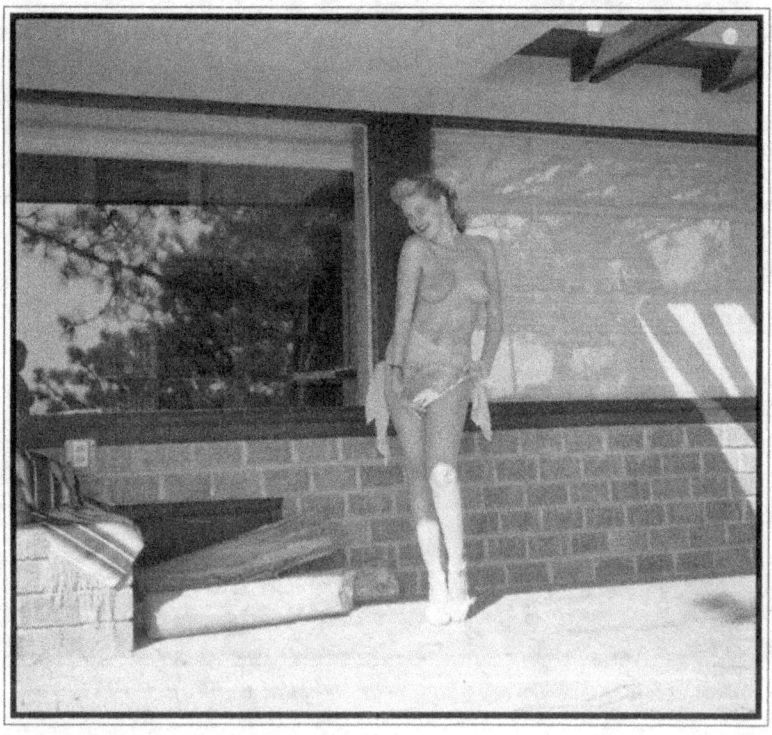

Minta, in front of Del Mar Studio, 1956.

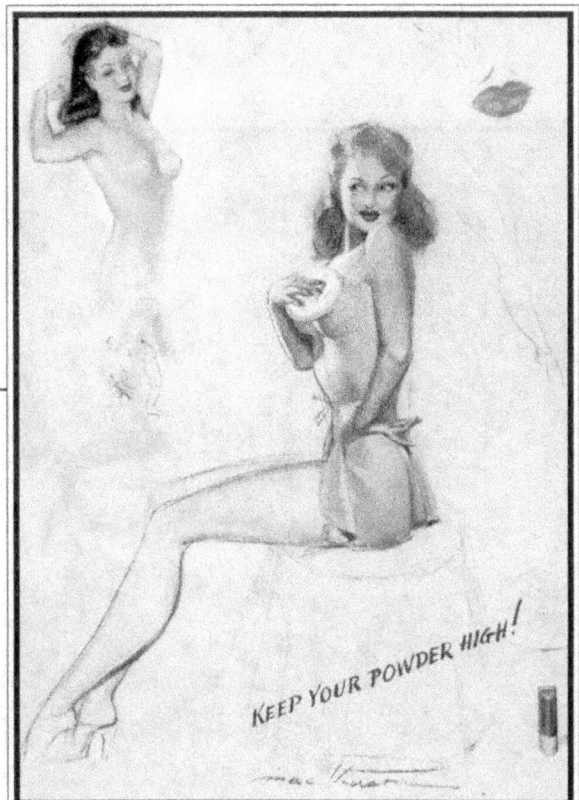

KEEP YOUR POWDER HIGH!

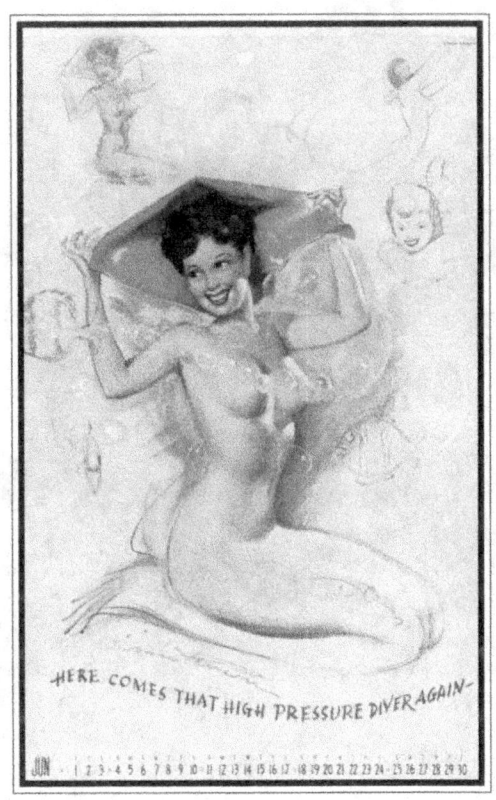

HERE COMES THAT HIGH PRESSURE DIVER AGAIN—

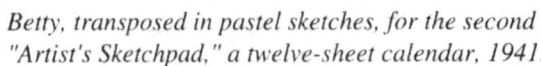

Betty, transposed in pastel sketches, for the second "Artist's Sketchpad," a twelve-sheet calendar, 1941.

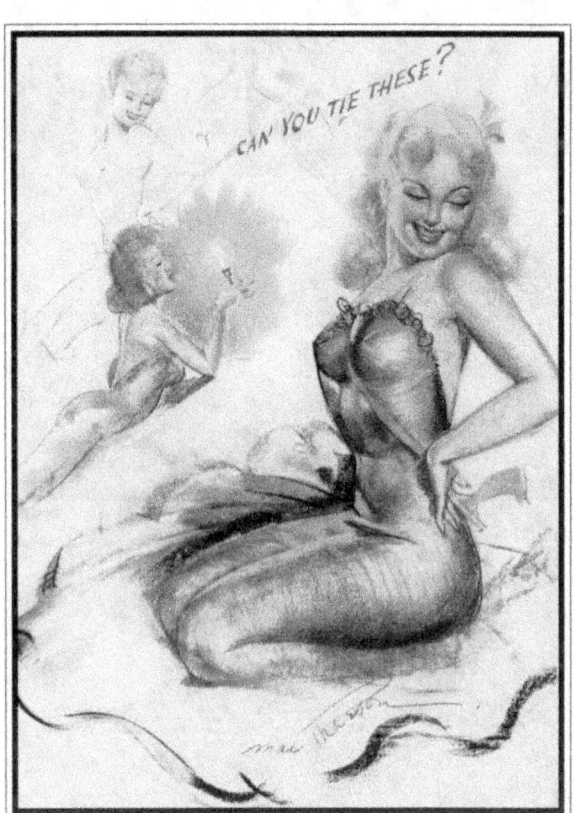

CAN YOU TIE THESE?

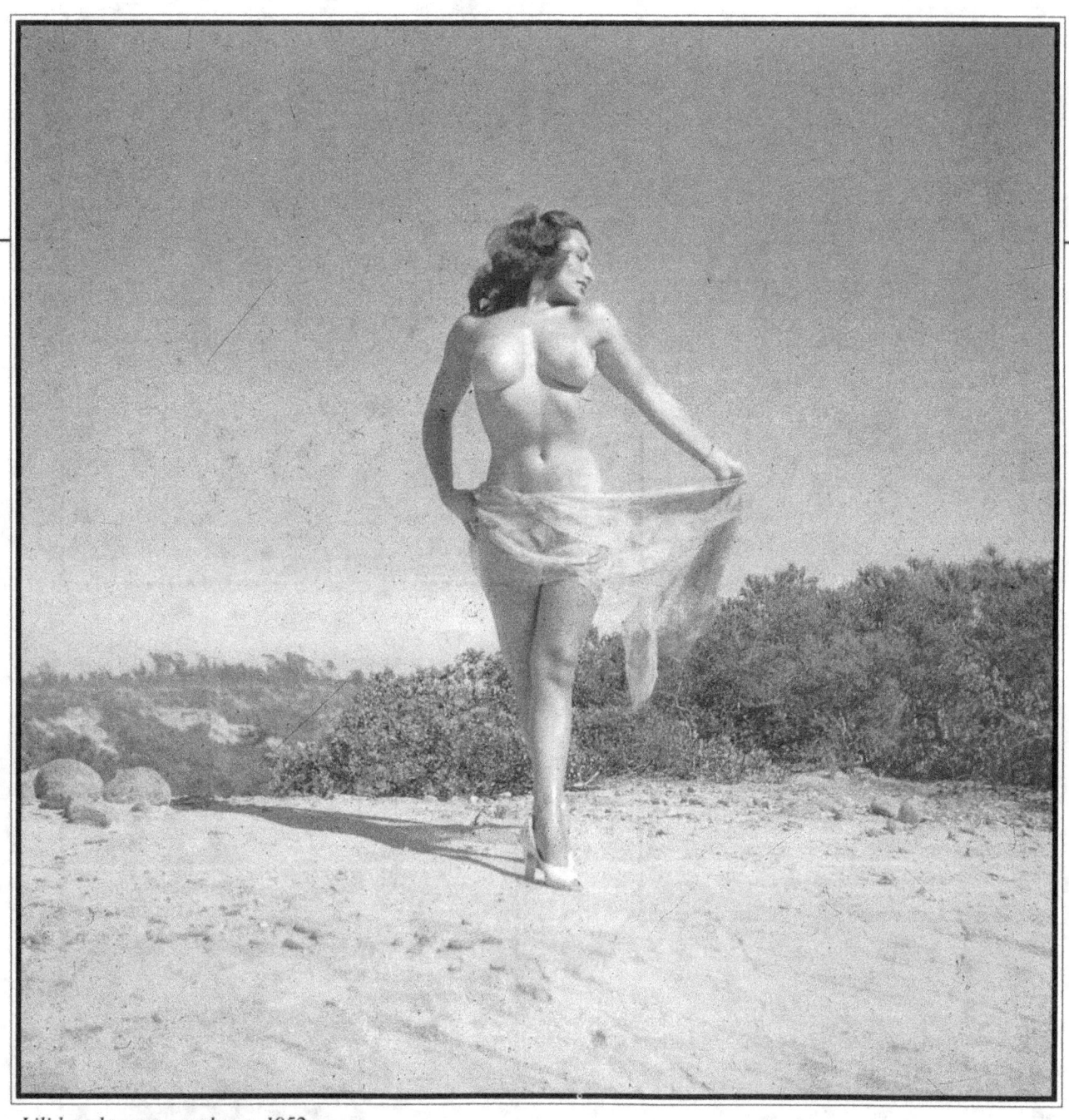

Lili loved to pose outdoors, 1952.

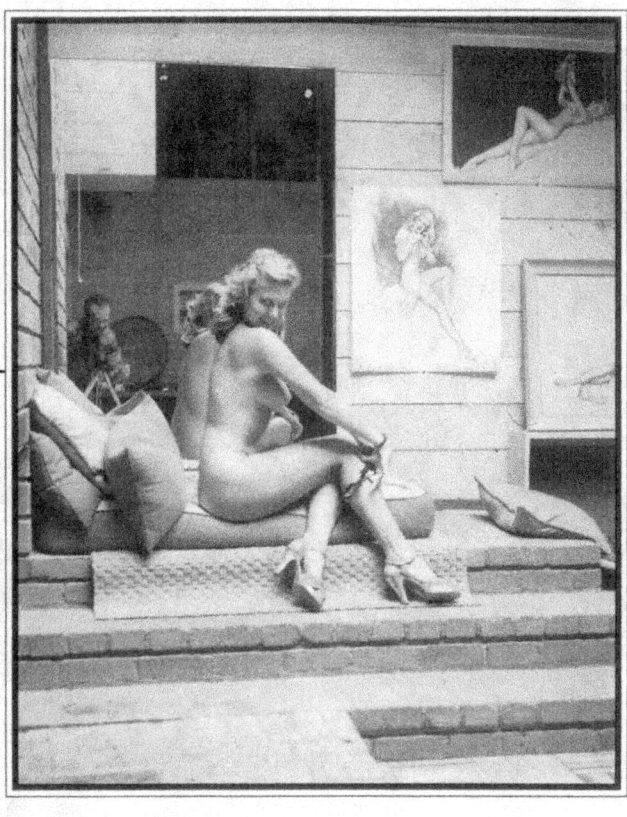

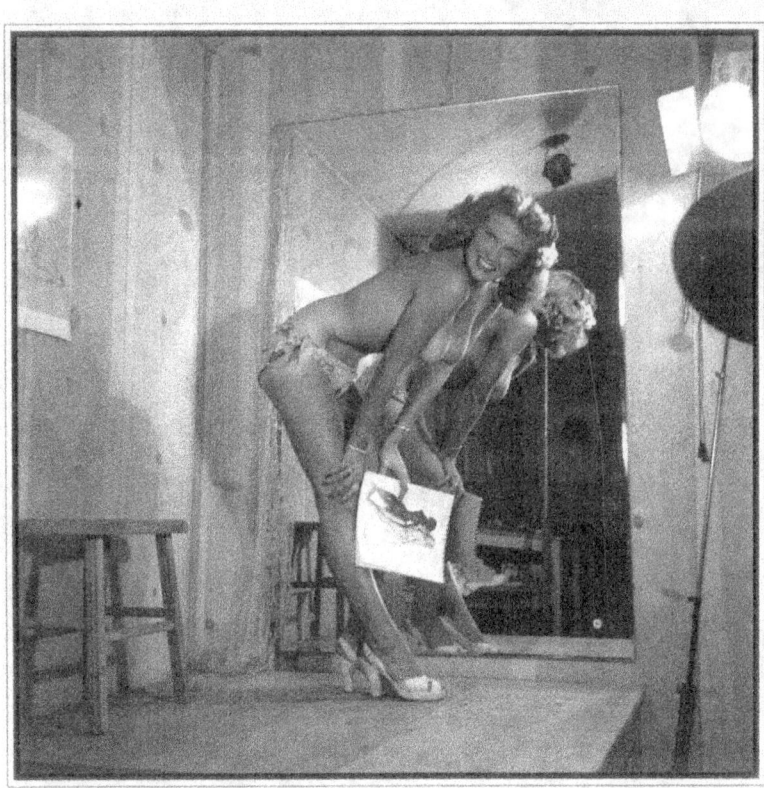

Minta preferred to pose indoors, 1947 to 1957.

23

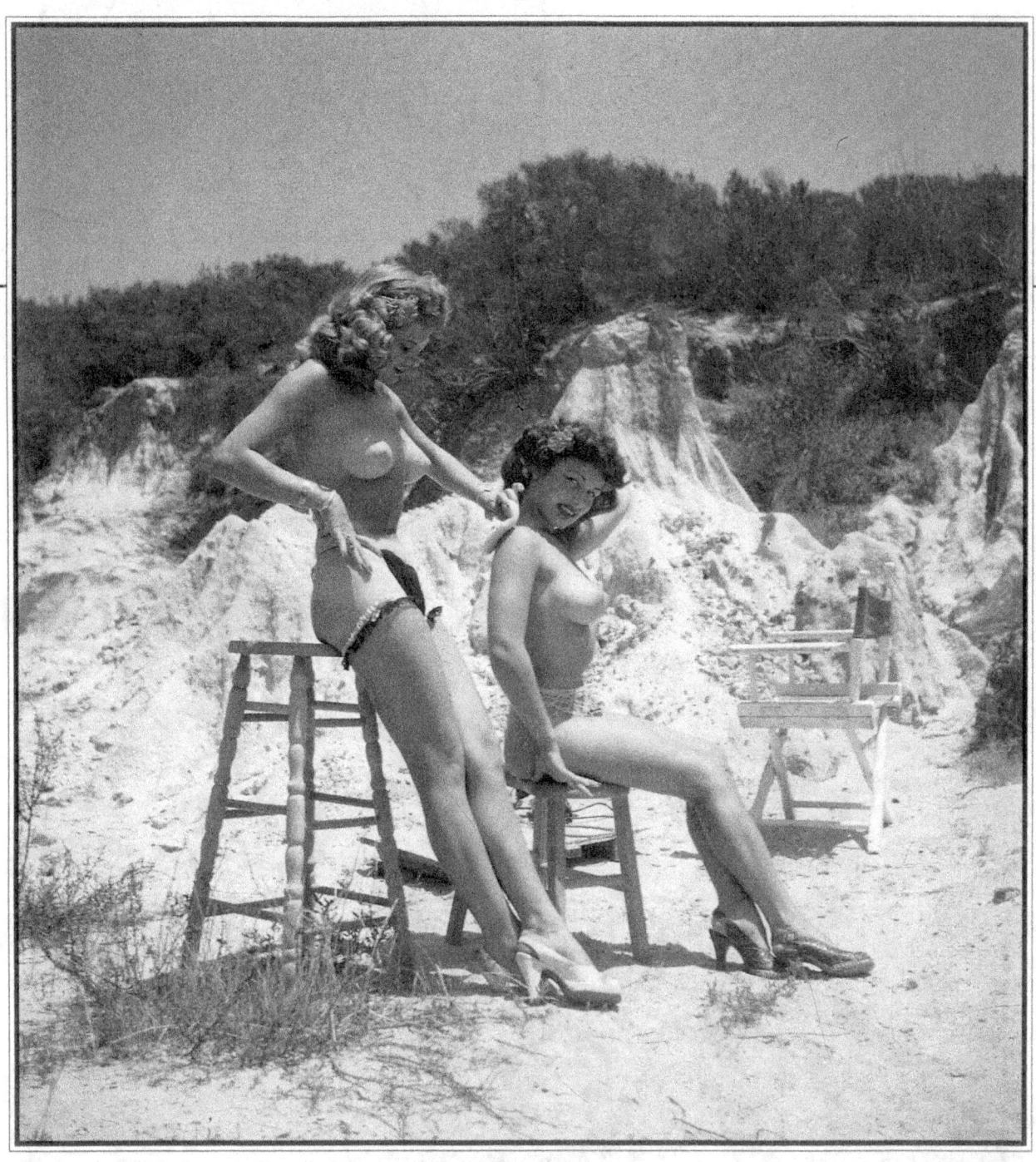

Minita and Lili "pretty up" for color photos.

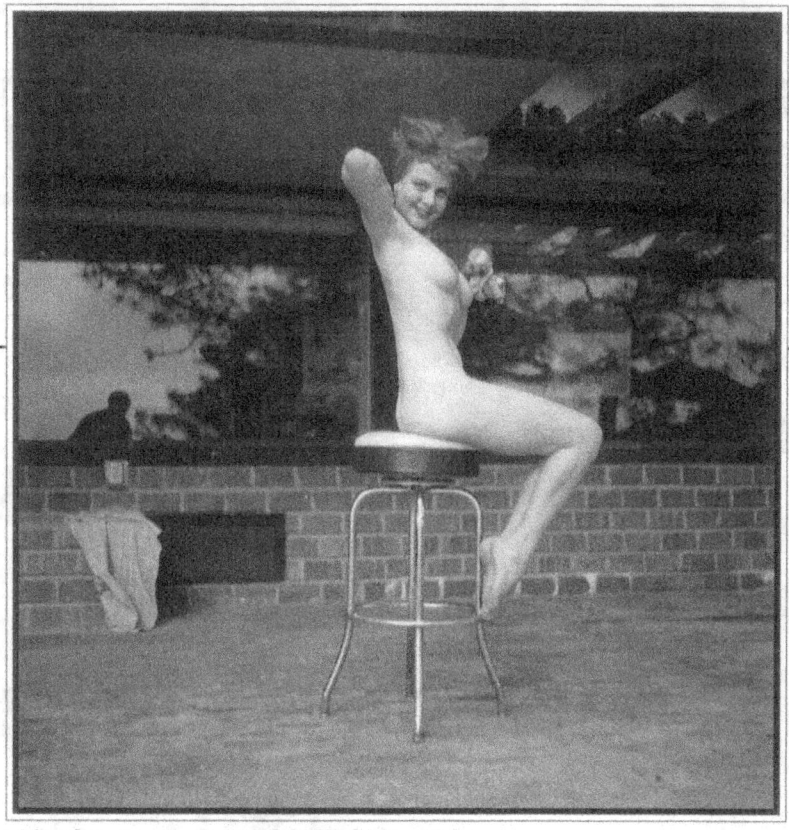

Marsha poses in front of the Del Mar studio.

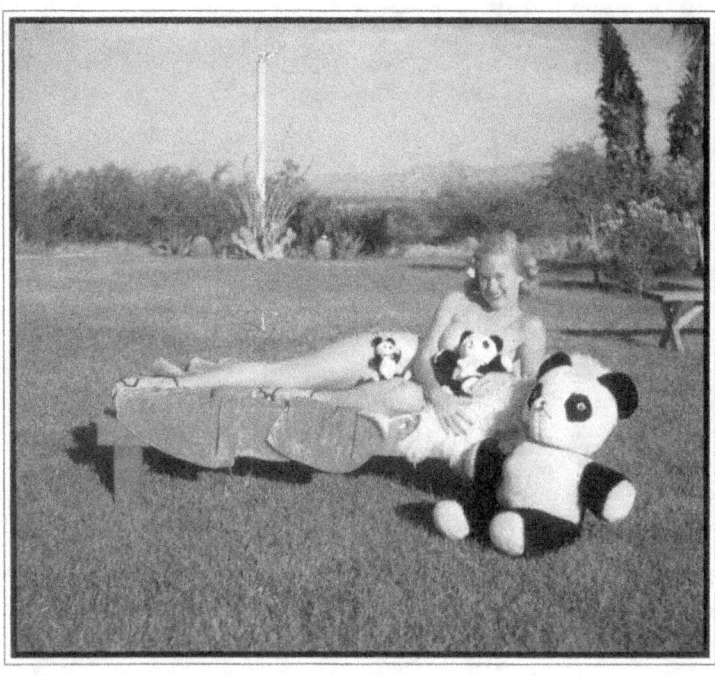

"Honey Bare," Scottsdale, Arizona, 1956.

25

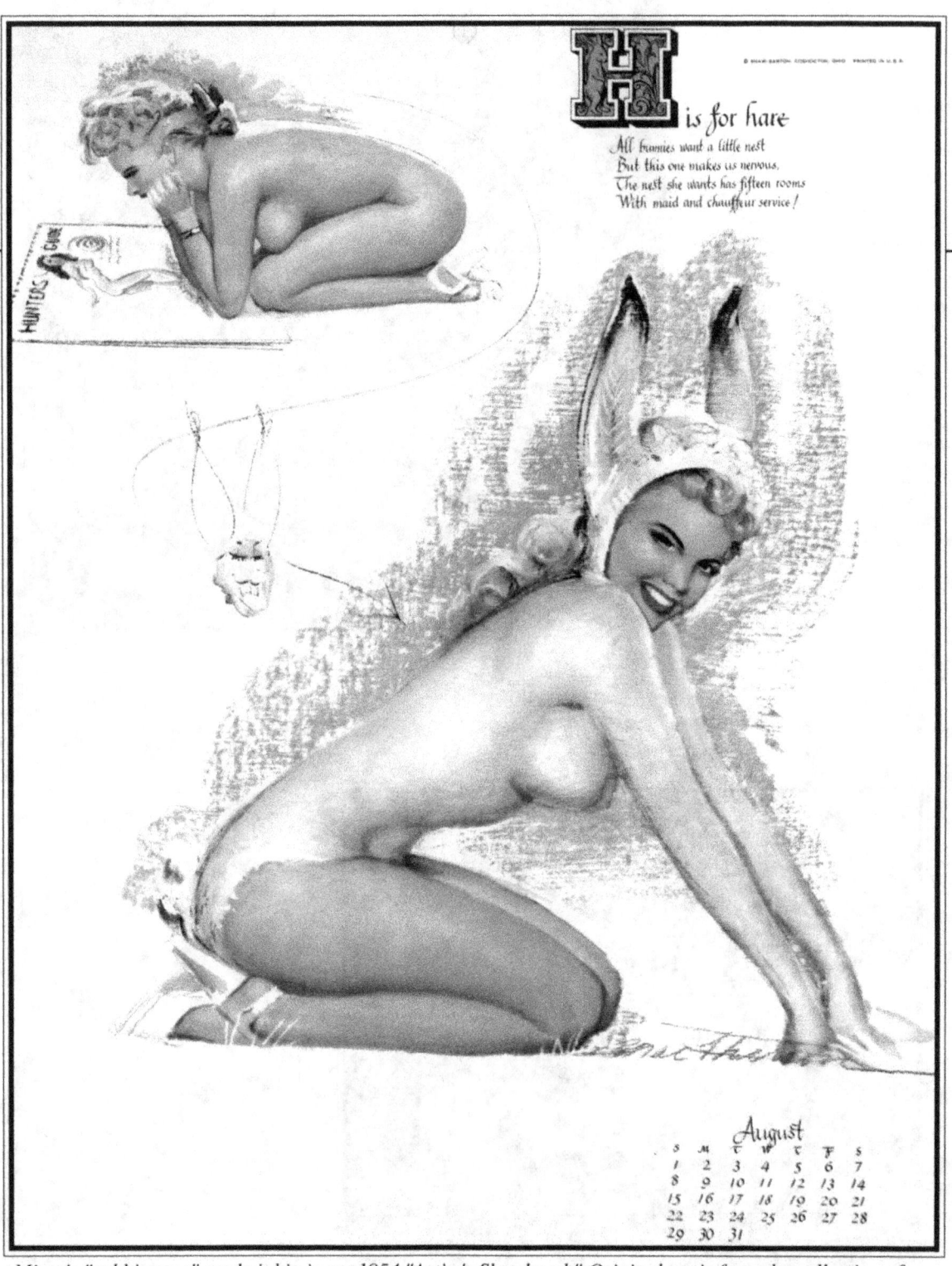

H is for hare

All bunnies want a little nest
But this one makes us nervous,
The nest she wants has fifteen rooms
With maid and chauffeur service!

August

S	M	T	W	T	F	S
	1	2	3	4	5	6	7
8	9	10	11	12	13	14
15	16	17	18	19	20	21
22	23	24	25	26	27	28
29	30	31				

Minta's "rabbit pose" made it big in my 1954 "Artist's Sketchpad." Original art is from the collection of Max and Barbara Collins.

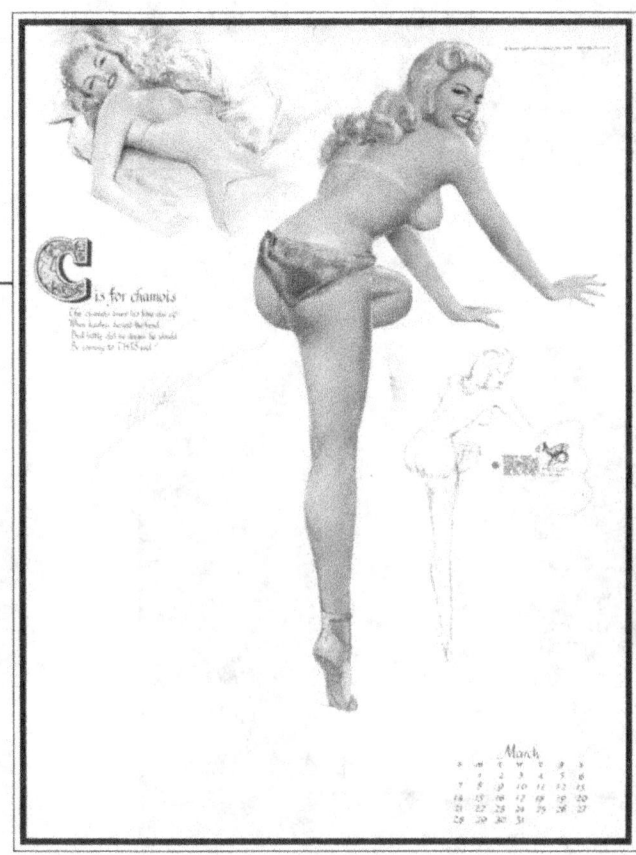

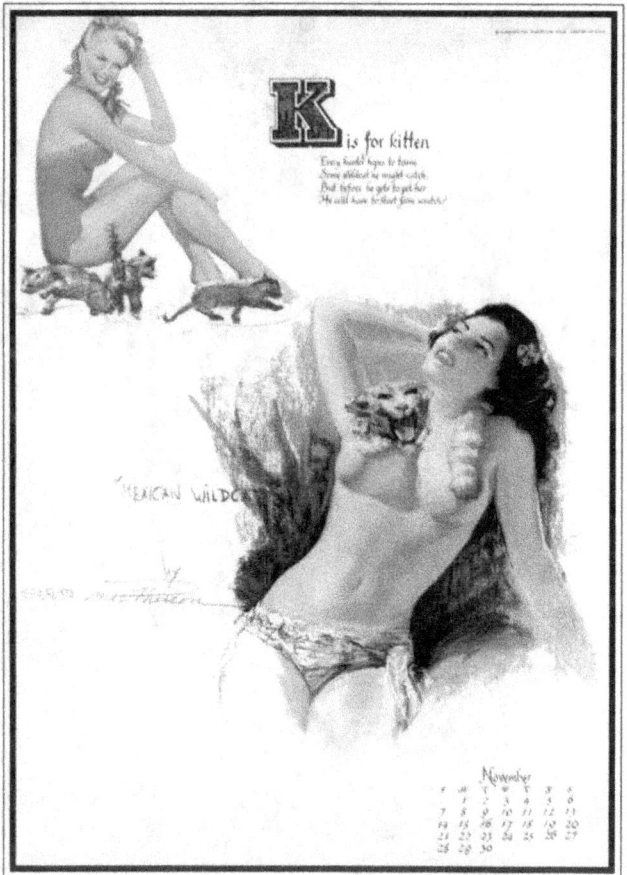

Two pages from "Hunter's Guide," an early Shaw–Barton twelve-sheet calendar.

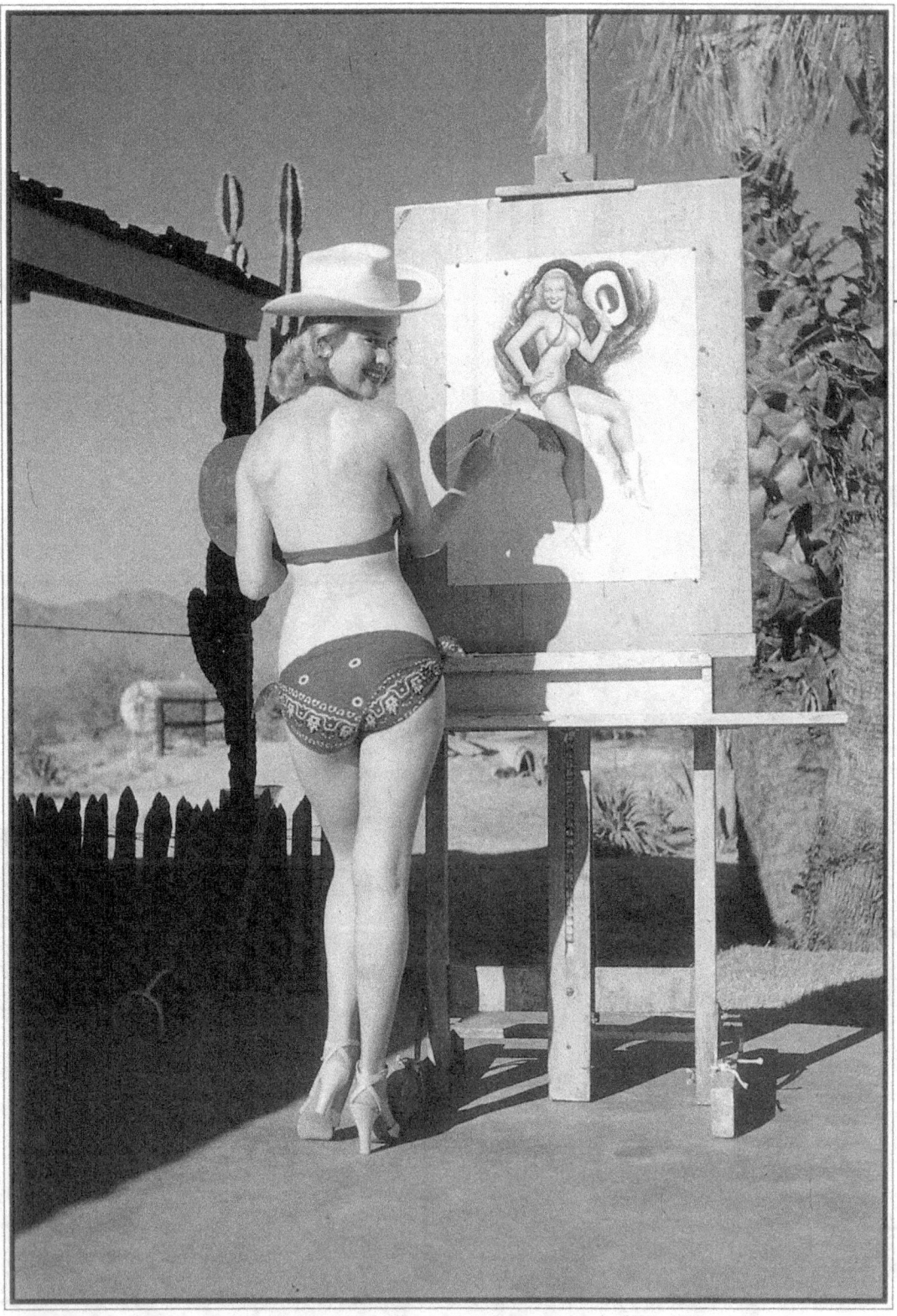

A Scottsdale fashion model with a cowgirl illustration from my book, "Fun Hunting."

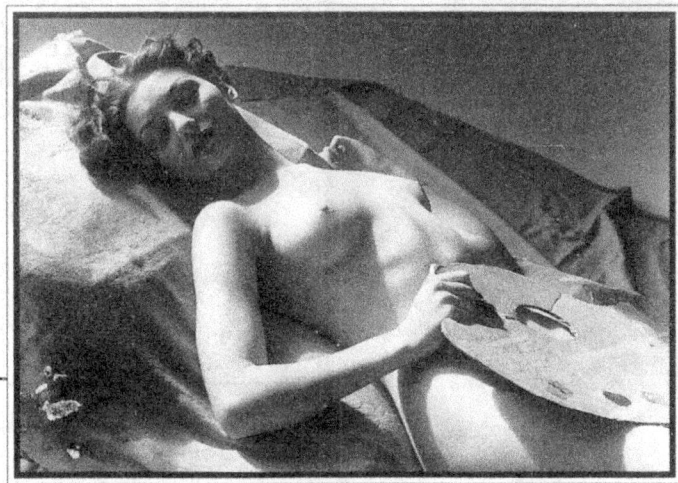

Minneapolis model, 1939.

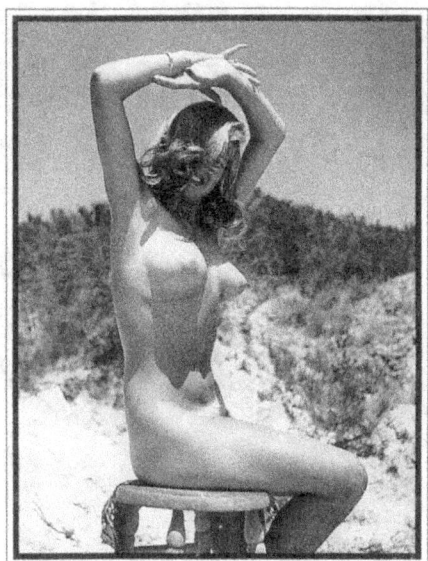

Minta Hoia, 1949.

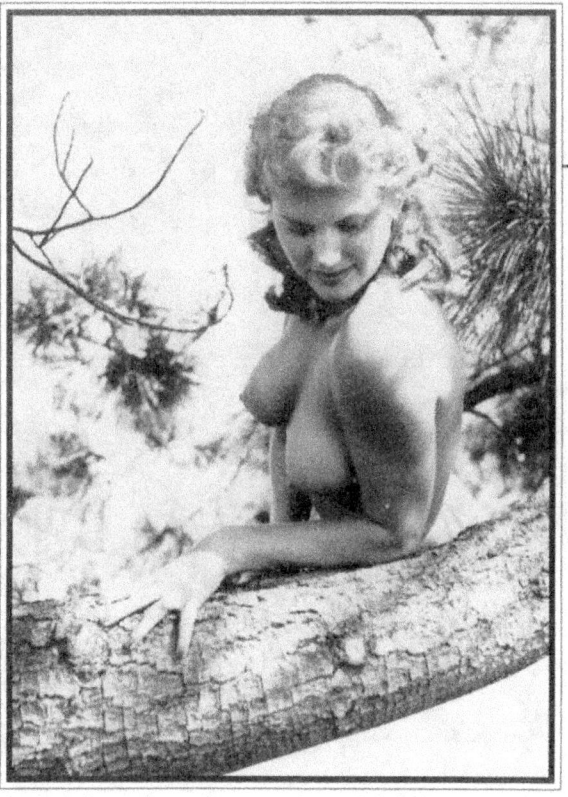

Minta, from the collection of Randolph Hunt.

At the home plant of Brown & Bigelow, Earl again met with Charlie Ward, then was introduced to Clair Fry, the art director. Fry assigned him to a small studio on the top floor, and took him on a tour of the plant.

"Clair showed me around the art department and I met the other artists and designers, all top men in the field. Afterwards, we had lunch together at a little restaurant in St. Paul. It was good to be with a group of professionals who treated me with the respect due an artist," says Earl.

Earl had much to learn about the calendar art business, but Clair Fry was quite willing to share all that he knew with the new employee of Brown & Bigelow.

"He was a friendly, slight man who knew more about art than anyone I'd ever met," says Earl of the art director.

However, Earl was a willing pupil and was working hard at his craft. It was good to have a steady income; Earl directed the accounting department to send a portion of his salary each week to Dianne for the care of Michael and Sylvia.

When the snows came that winter, Frank Van Keuren departed again for sunny California, taking his wife with him, and leaving the house to Earl and the family dog. After work, Earl would take the dog and go for long walks along the river, as he still didn't know that many people in St. Paul, except at work, which was going well.

"I teamed up with Ray Stoneman, a young executive at the plant. Ray had a friend who had a list of some of the most beautiful girls in the St. Paul-Minneapolis area. Together, Ray and I screened them, and came up with a luscious collection of potential models, as pretty as any I had seen since the Earl Carroll Girls. In fact, these Minnesota girls had a more natural beauty about them."

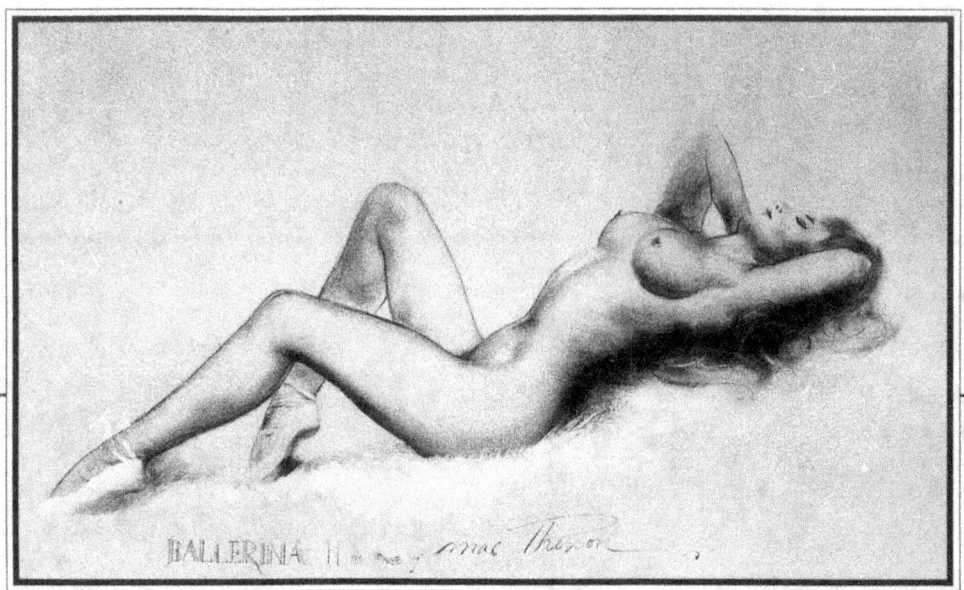

Annette.

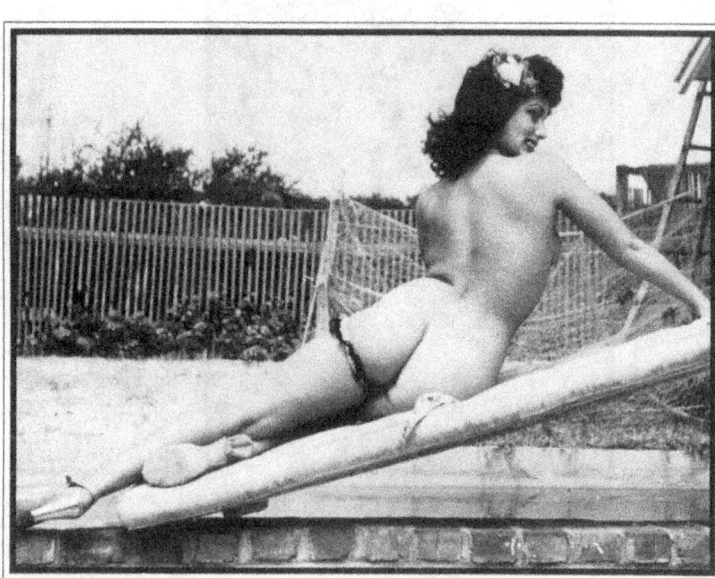

Lili, by the ranch pool, 1946.

Earl would photograph the girls at the Van Keuren home, which was ideal for the purpose, and make sketches from the photos at the studio. From these sketches, he would be able to paint.

"Clair was pleased with my work, but none of it had been used as yet on a calendar. He cautioned me to be patient. I didn't realize it, but I was soon to meet the model who would earn me a place on the next calendar," says Earl.

One evening, Earl was sitting by the fire with the dog beside him, when the phone rang.

"Mr. MacPherson, my name is Annette Flowers. I am a Minneapolis model. I am twenty years old. My measurements are 34-24-34. I weigh 110 lbs. and I have red hair. What else do you want to know?" the caller said.

"Why are you calling me?" Earl asked.

"Because I'd like a job modeling for you," Annette replied.

"Come on over," said Earl.

"Twenty minutes later, I opened the door into the first blizzard of the season and twenty of the happiest years of my life," recalls Earl.

Annette was very beautiful and businesslike. She arrived with a full portfolio of modeling photographs which she had done so far in her career. Earl says:

"Annette had a provocative smile and a fine figure in a bathing suit. She wore clothes with a distinct flair. I questioned her with, 'Miss Flowers, have you ever done any nude modeling?'"

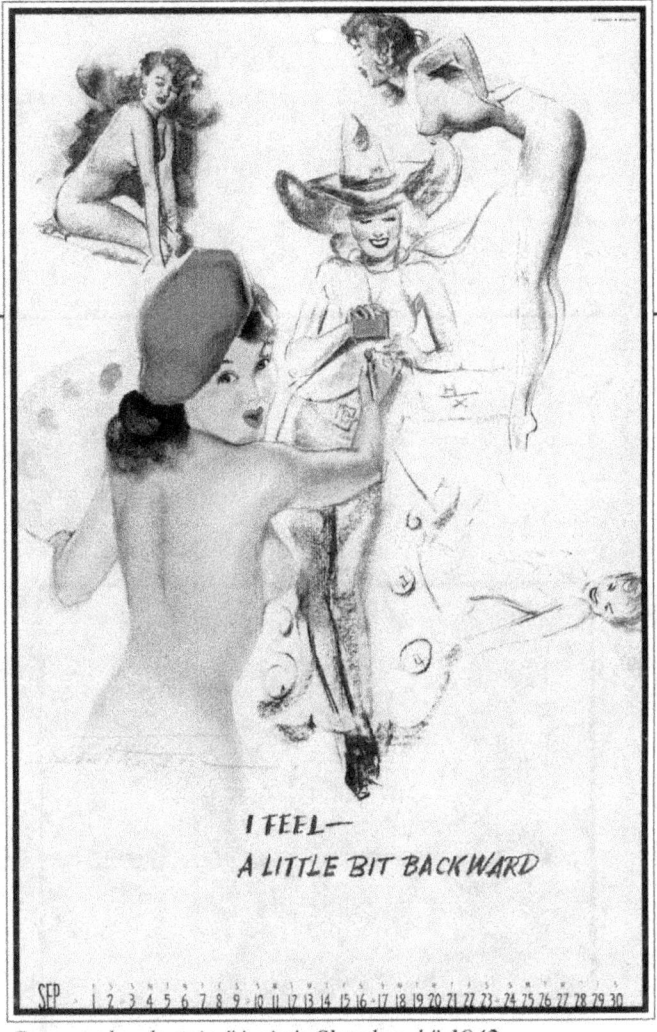

I FEEL—
A LITTLE BIT BACKWARD

Betty, at her best in "Artist's Sketchpad," 1942.

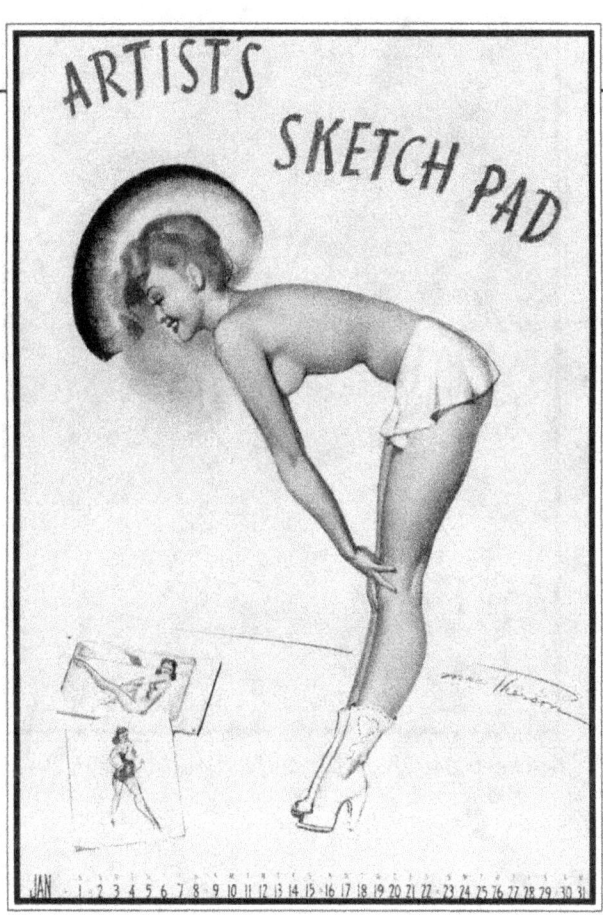

ARTIST'S
SKETCH PAD

"'Only in front of my mirror,' she replied, with a twinkle in her eye.
"'How'd you look?' I asked
"'Terrific!' she said."
Earl was interested, in more ways than one. He used Annette to model for the first "Artist's Sketch Pad," a new twelve sheet pin-up calendar, published by Brown & Bigelow the next year. It was a series of sketches, with little side sketches showing how the sketches were done, all printed on brown butcher's paper. Clair Fry was tremendously pleased with the result: it became a best seller in the 1941 line. This also made Charlie Ward very happy, especially when "The Artist's Sketch Book" earned one million dollars for the company.
Meanwhile, Annette and Earl had become very much involved with each other. Earl stopped his correspondence with Lorraine, knowing that he had no plans to return to California, not now anyway.
"I told Annette that I had been married and was waiting for my divorce to be final. She understood, taking me home to meet her family. When the six months were up, Annette and I were married," says Earl.

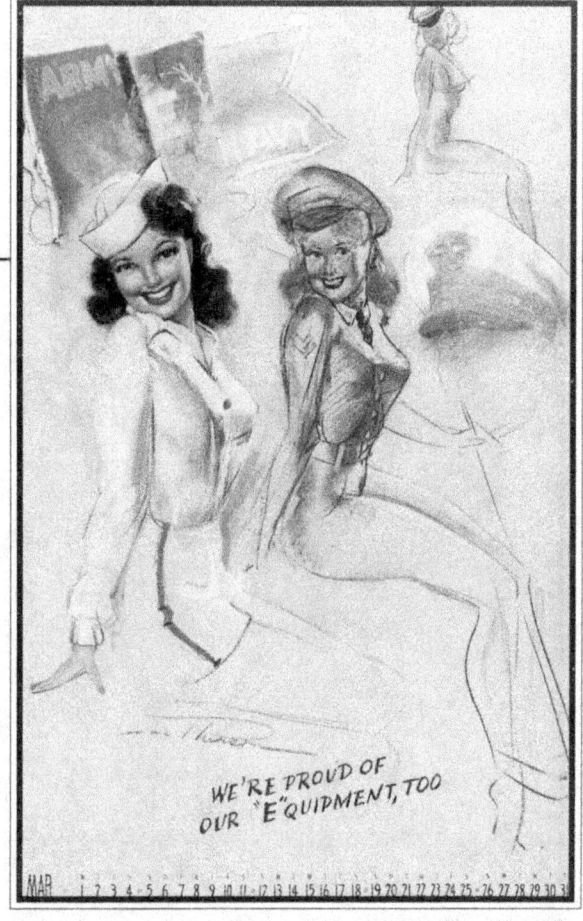

Betty gets patriotic and ready for World War II, 1942.

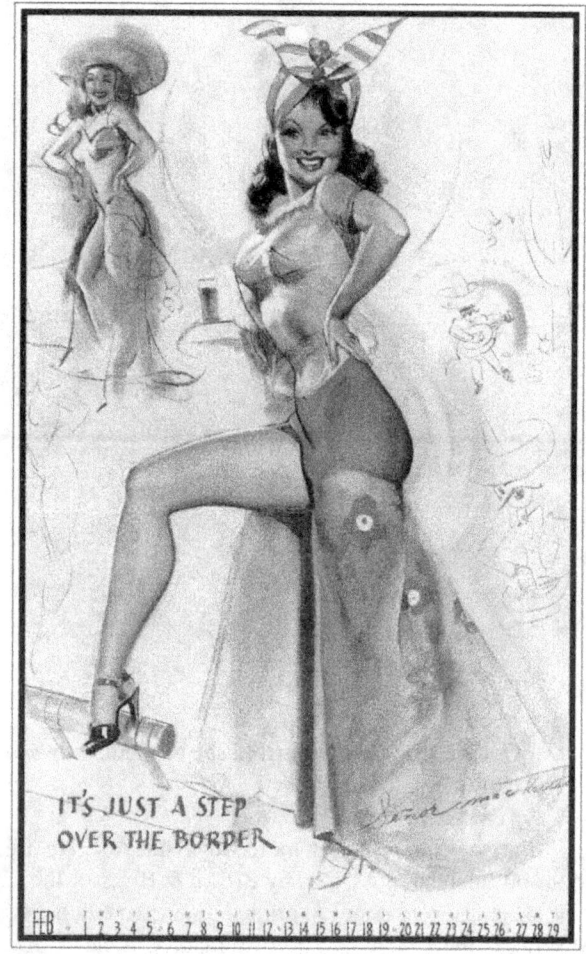

Betty travels to Mexico, 1942.

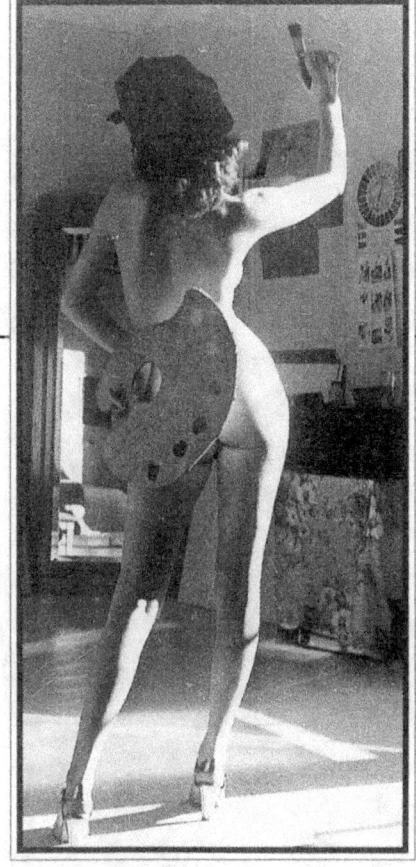

Anette poses for the cover of my first "Artist's Sketchbook..."

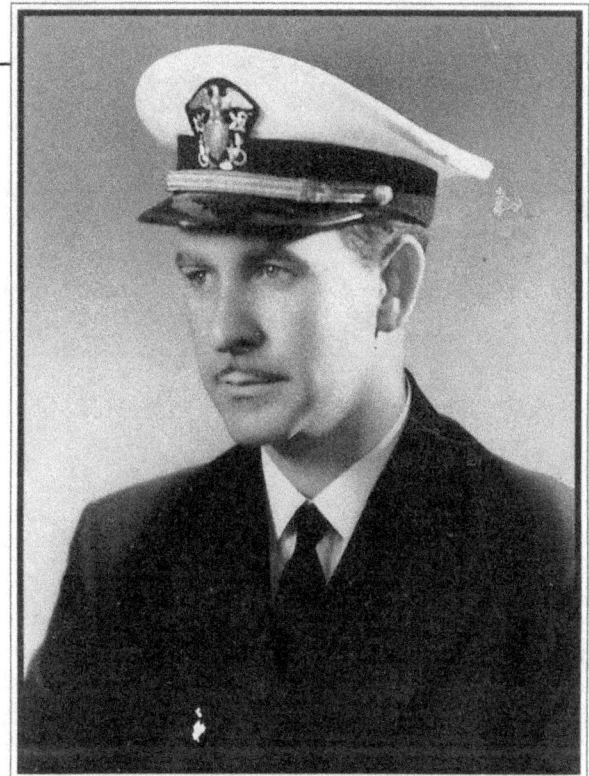

... and so does Ensign Earl MacPherson, U.S.N.R., 1942.

"I was making it big. I had a gorgeous red-haired bride. My future had never looked brighter. I began work on the second 'Artist's Sketch Pad,' with Annette as my constant model and lover. It was December, 1941. I didn't realize that I would soon have to put my art career on hold and spend almost four years in the United States Navy, as a lieutenant, teaching plane recognition to would-be pilots," remembers Earl.

Earl was lucky. Years previously, he had painted the portraits of Nelson Howard's children, not long after doing those of President Hoover's grandchildren. Howard was now a lieutenant and procurement officer for the Navy. He arranged for Earl to attend special training classes at Dartmouth College, in order to become a commissioned officer. Eventually, Annette was able to join Earl at the Ohio Naval Training Center, where he worked for the next two years, teaching recognition through the use of sketches and slides.

"In the afternoon, a lot of students would go to sleep in the darkened classroom," comments Earl. "That problem was overcome by sneaking slides of my former nude models in with the ships and planes."

Brown & Bigelow had come out with the second "Artist's Sketch Pad," which Earl had hurried to finish before getting inducted. Now Annette and Earl had a production of their own—a new baby son. Brian was born in Ohio, just before his Dad was transferred.

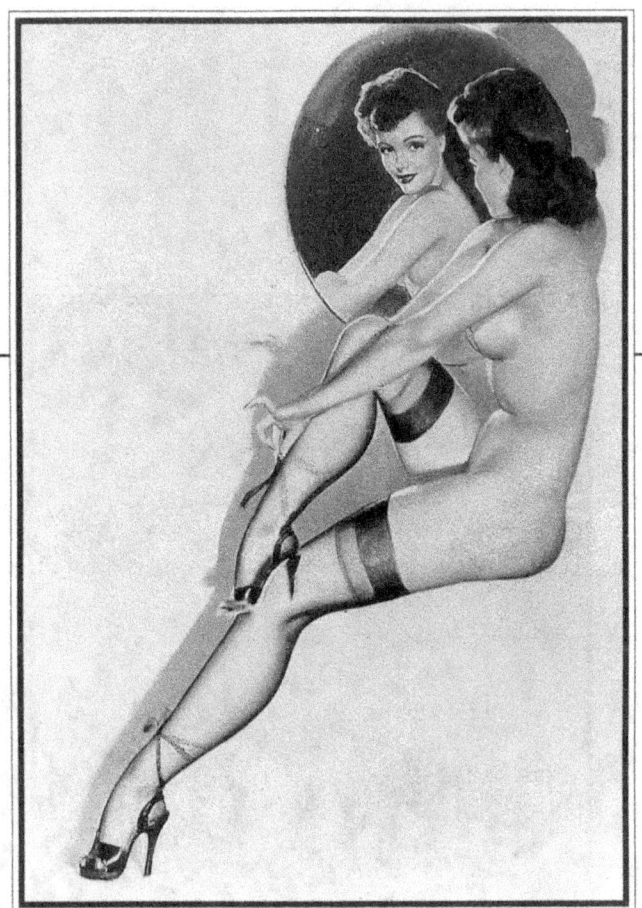

As part of my duties as a naval officer, I painted huge pin-ups for the Ward Room.

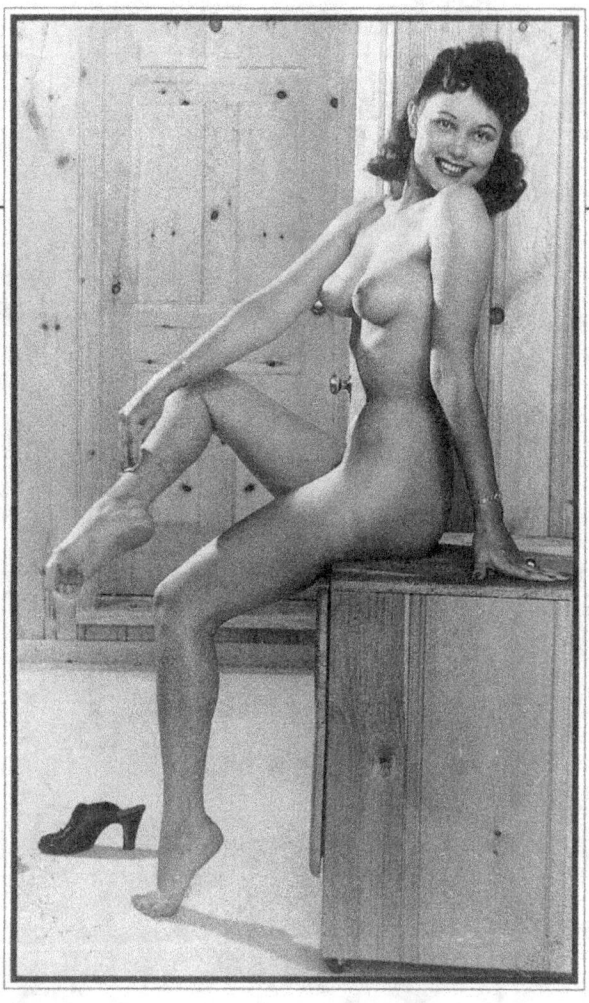

Earl was sent by the Bureau of Aeronautics to the Navy's largest flying base in Jacksonville, Florida. Annette and the baby joined him, as soon as he was able to find housing for them. Housing turned out to be a beautiful old white colonial mansion on the St. John's river, owned by the widow of the former president of the Reynold's tobacco company. Earl, using his talents of persuasion, convinced the widow to rent him the estate (which she only used on weekends) at reasonable cost in exchange for him painting portraits of her two daughters. Annette, Earl and Brian spent the next two years living in the luxurious home.

While stationed in Ohio, Earl had been approached by representatives of Shaw-Barton, a new calendar company that had been started by former employees of Brown & Bigelow. As the war ended, he was contacted again by them.

Living in Florida had spoiled the young family. Rather than face the cold winters of Minnesota, they decided to seek their fortunes in Earl's adopted state of California. This would be possible if Earl went to work for Shaw-Barton. The new company had no restrictions on where their employees lived, unlike Charlie Ward, who had insisted that all the B&B workers live in Minnesota.

Earl left the Navy with the rank of lieutenant and with his family departed for the West Coast in a secondhand trailer, painted battleship gray using government leftovers.

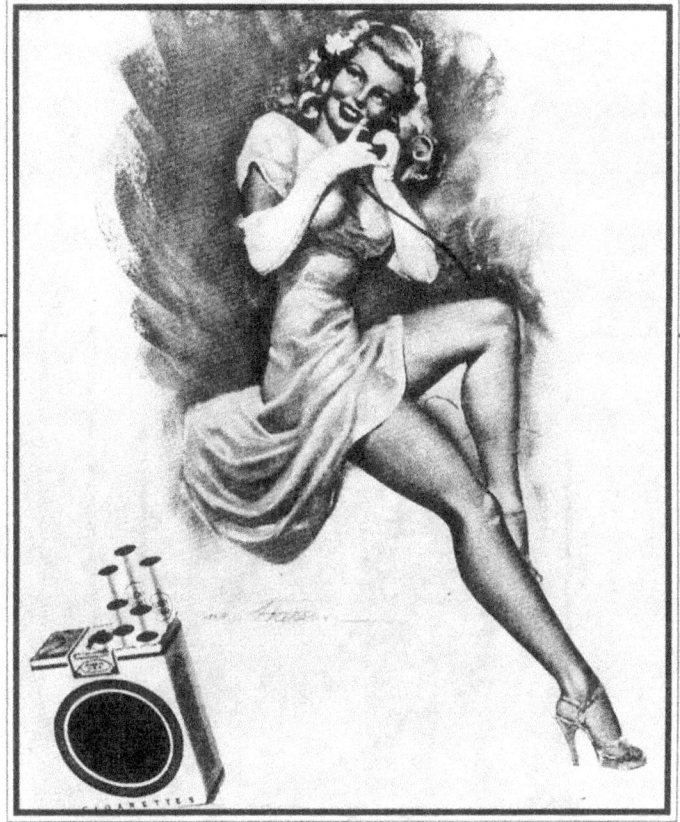

After the war, I made it "BIG" with a "Lucky Strike" calendar...

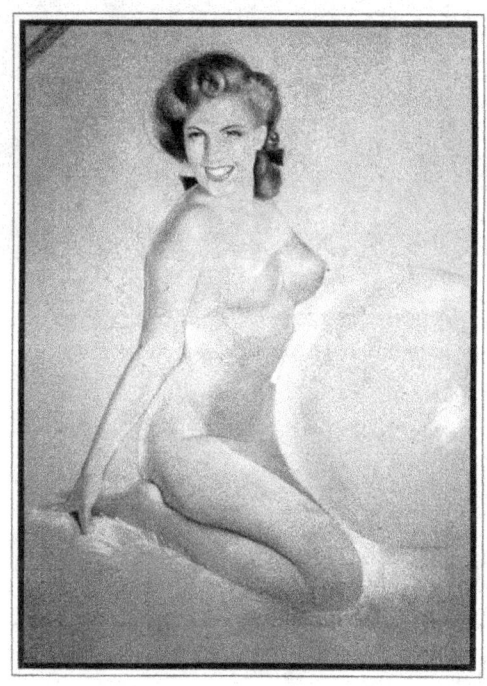

... and a Walter Foster book on pin-up art, 1954.

"After a leisurely trip through the South, with stops in Phoenix and Palm Springs, we settled in Laguna Beach for the summer. One weekend, we drove to Big Bear to see Mom, Dad, Michael and Sylvia. Upon arrival, I learned that Dianne had taken the children to live in San Francisco with Mary Lee, her sister, who had married a Navy captain," says Earl.

That fall, Earl, Annette and their son stayed in La Jolla with Commander Bob Dose and his family. Dose had been Earl's second-in-command at the base in Jacksonville, and they had become very close friends. When Earl received six thousand dollars from Shaw-Barton for his third "Artist's Sketch Pad" (the first for them), he used it as a down payment on a four-acre lime and avocado ranch in Del Mar, California.

On the ranch, Earl built a studio facing a small reservoir which was made into a swimming pool. It was here that Earl had the most productive year of his art career. Annette, busy with Brian and the ranch, suggested that Earl use all the other models he wanted. She helped train the young models and made colorful posing props for them to use.

Earl's first calendar sketch pad for Shaw-Barton sold well. He painted a series of twelve pin-ups for blotters and another feature's calendar for them. Earl also did "Going Places," which was used by Lucky Strike for advertising.

"There was more to painting the beautiful pin-ups than met the eye. The models had to be taught to assume poses that were graceful and provocative, but not too sexy. They had to learn camera angles so that their poses would show off their voluptuous curves and yet not be overly suggestive. I learned to speed up my production by taking colored photos of the nude models in the sand arroyos behind the studio, where there was a lot of reflected light to fill in the shadows," says Earl.

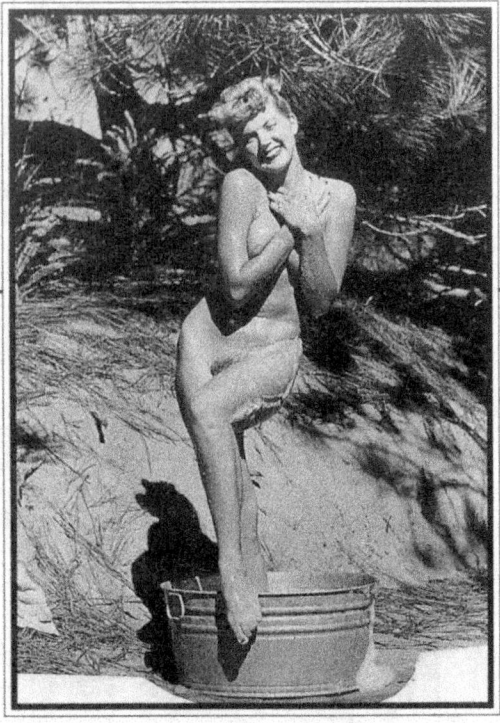

Minta was a very "clean" model.

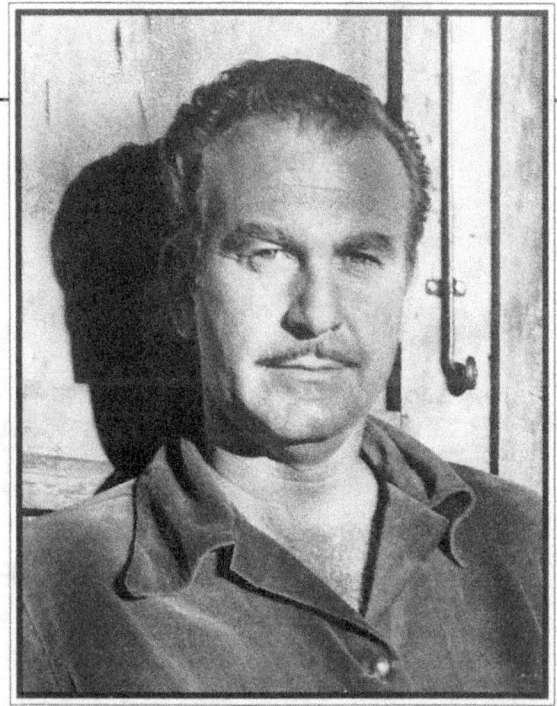

The artist, me, at San Miguel de Allende, Mexico, c. 1955,...

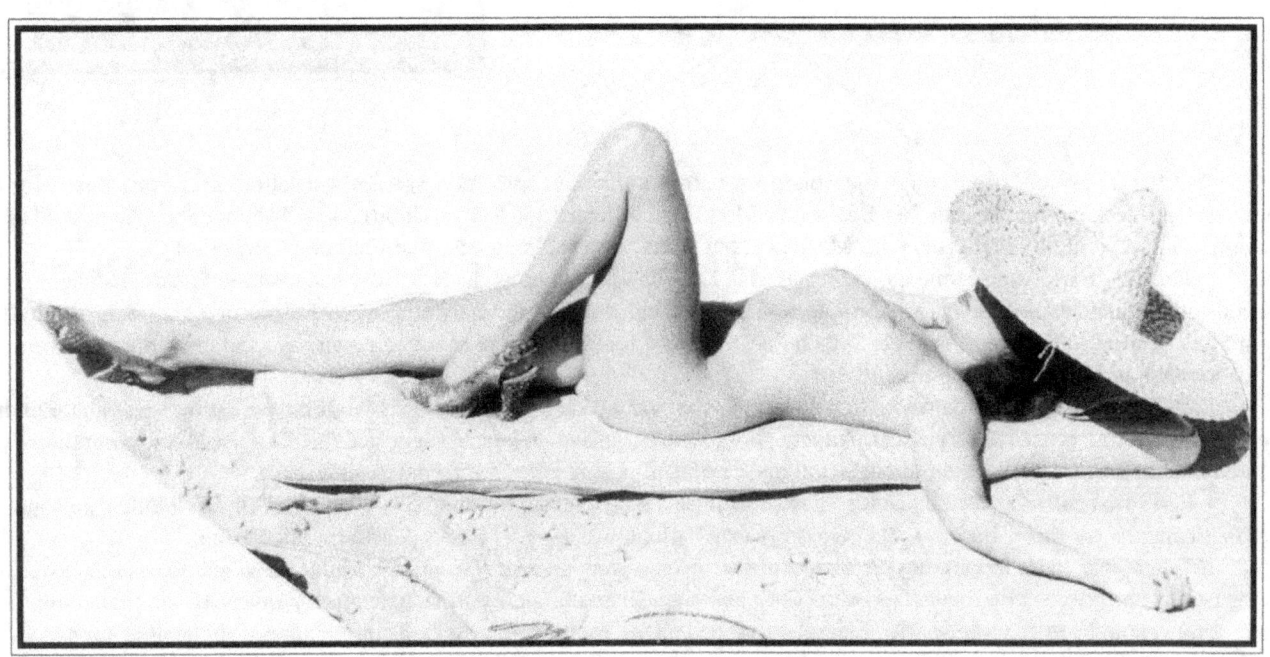

... and a bit of local color.

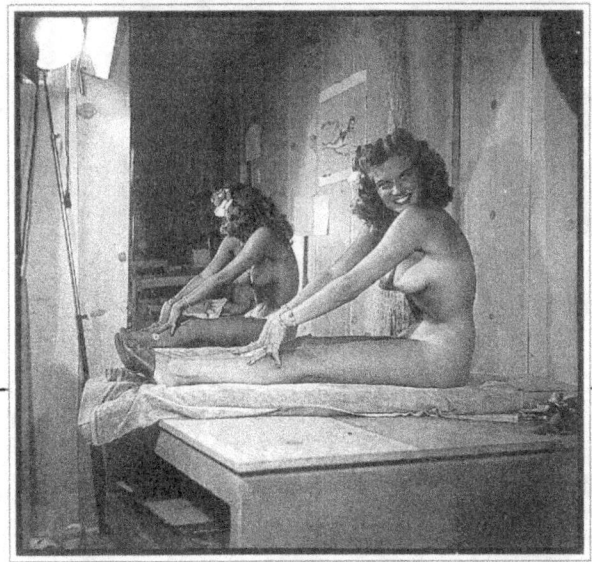

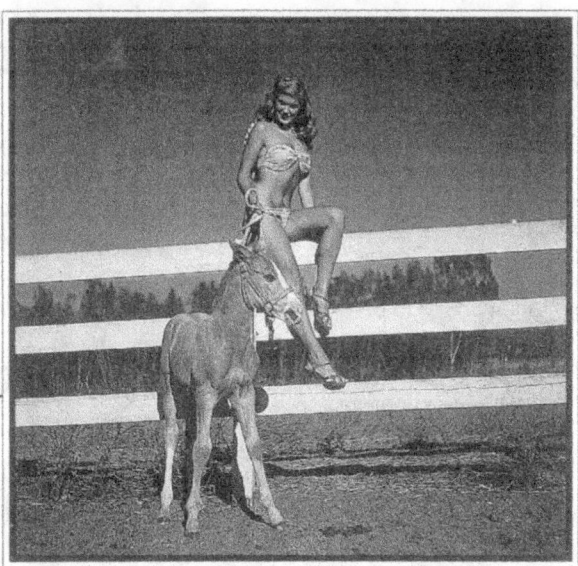

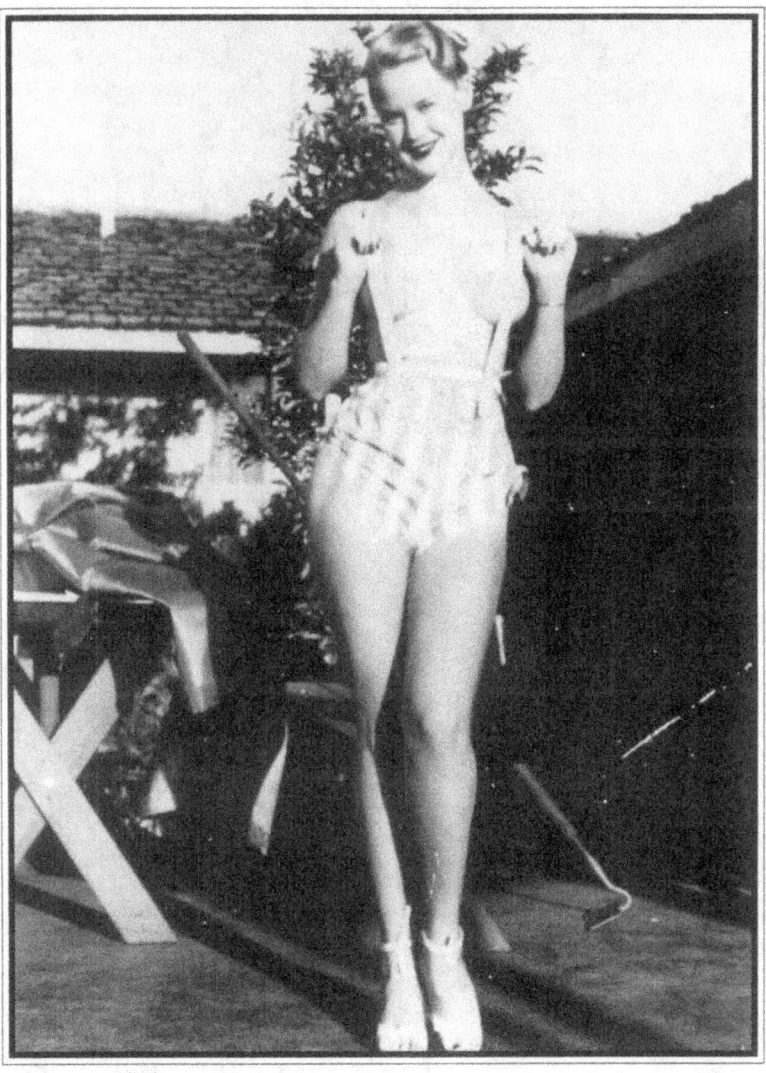

Dianne, 1932.

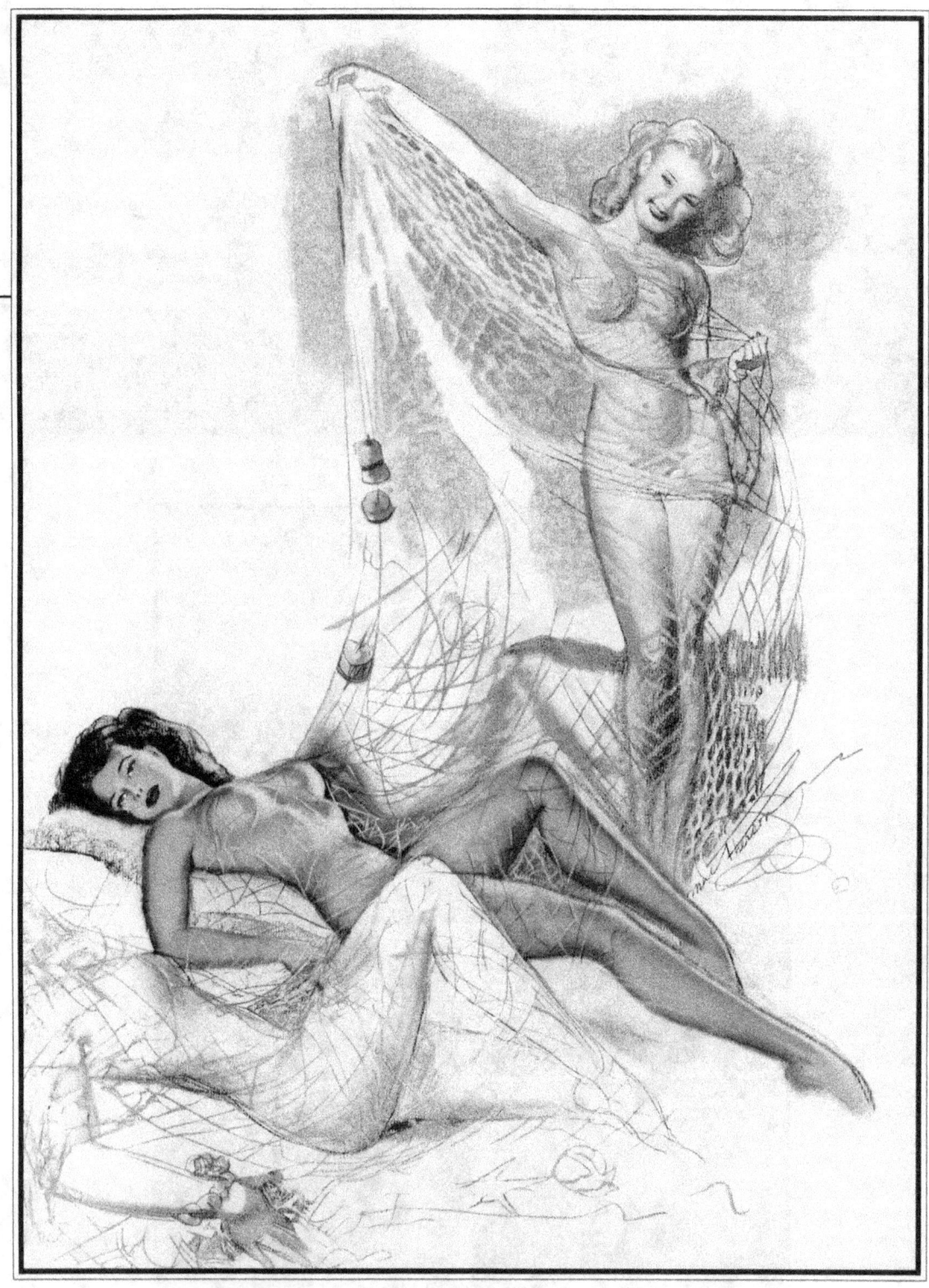

The fisherman's daughters.

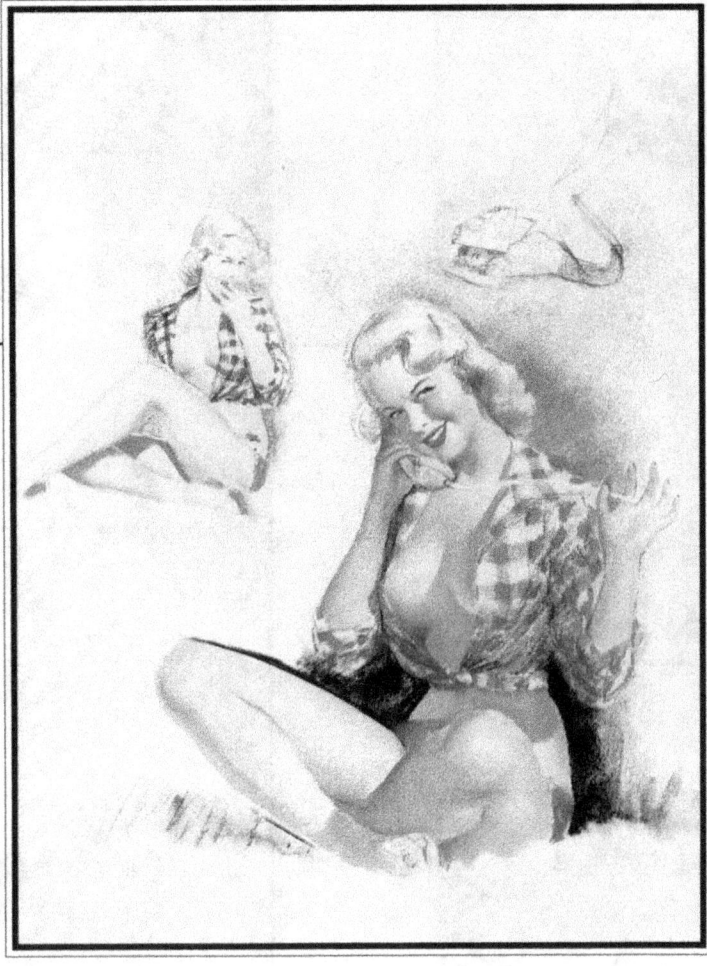

*"Fun Hunting" lass,
Scottsdale, 1950.*

Using the photos to select the best poses, Earl would finish the sketches from life, in the studio. Bob Dose had discovered Lillian, the brunette model Earl first began using. He comments:

"One day, she brought a sixteen-year-old blonde girlfriend, with the unlikely name of Minta Hoia, to pose with her. The blonde was unbelievably endowed with the natural assets needed in pin-up art. I began using both models together and they tried to out do each other in trying to please me."

The results were fantastic. Earl became the star artist at Shaw-Barton, whereas he had only been one of two dozen top calendar artists at Brown & Bigelow. Shaw-Barton paid his expenses to sales conventions, and sales and royalties on his pin-ups soared. Earl did a total of nine "Artist Sketch Pads" for Shaw-Barton over the years. In 1954, he came out with the "Fun Hunting Book," a parody with the pin-up girls dressed as various hunting birds.

Annette's parents joined her, Brian and Earl on the ranch, buying a half-interest in it, which Earl used to pay off his G.I. loan. Soon after that, Annette and Earl went driving in the hills above Del Mar where they saw a sand-colored dwelling that seemed to blend into the hillside.

"We stopped to admire the home and were asked in to see it by an attractive middle-aged blonde. She turned out to be the wife of the owner and architect, John Lloyd Wright, son of the famous architect Frank Lloyd Wright. Annette and I persuaded him to design a new home for us," says Earl.

"It was built in Torrey Pines Terrace, a new subdivision in the sandstone cliffs covered with rare Torrey pines that overlooked the blue Pacific Ocean. John's plan included a huge studio-living room with an enormous fireplace with steps at its base, which would serve as a model stand. The studio and a terrace faced the sea, to the west to catch the glorious sunsets," explains Earl.

"From the terrace, a path led beneath the pines to a small, contured, sand-colored pool. The bedrooms were built on a split-level floor above, with their own private patio. It was perfection, except for the hassles we encountered trying to get it built," he continues.

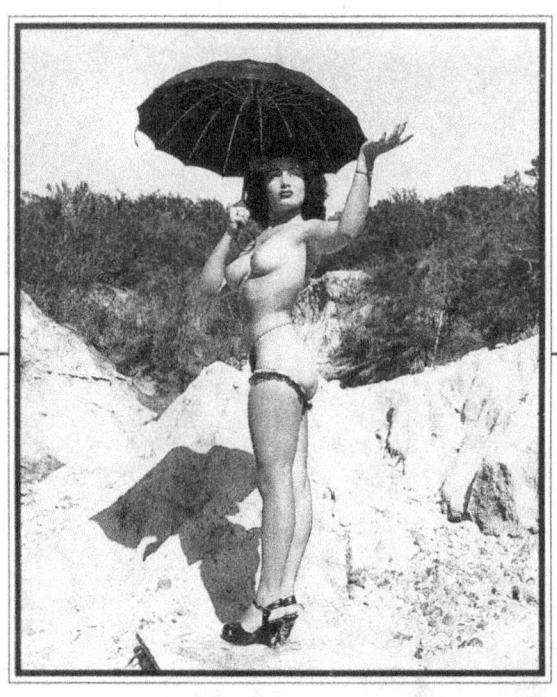

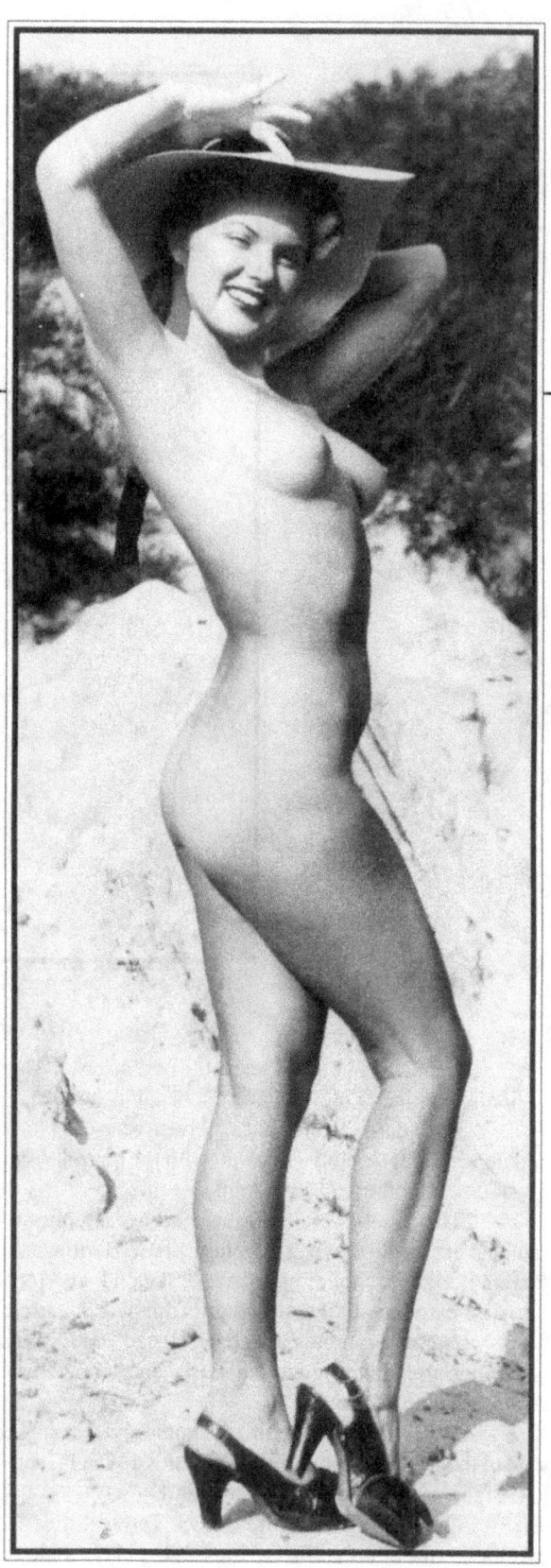

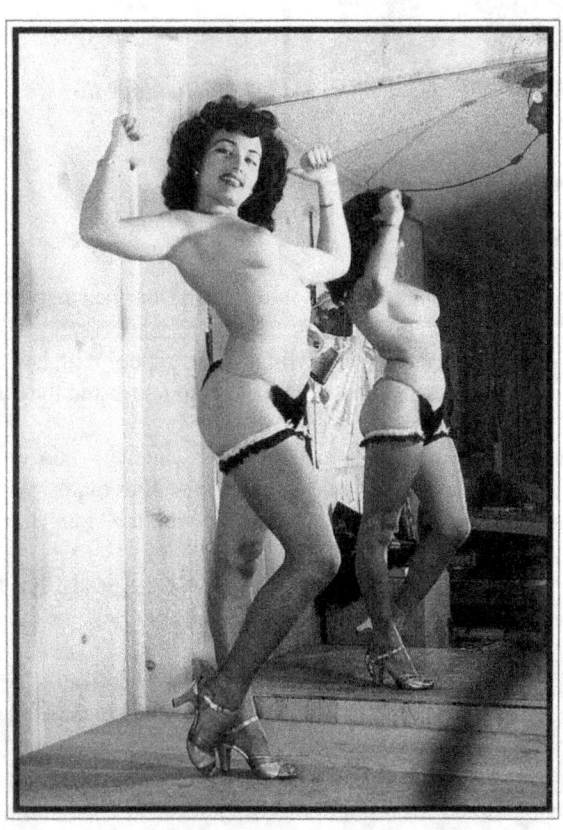

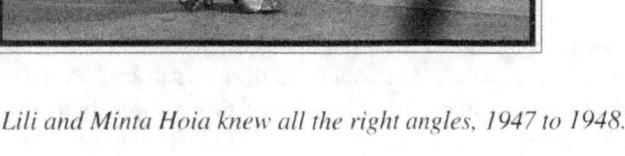

Lili and Minta Hoia knew all the right angles, 1947 to 1948.

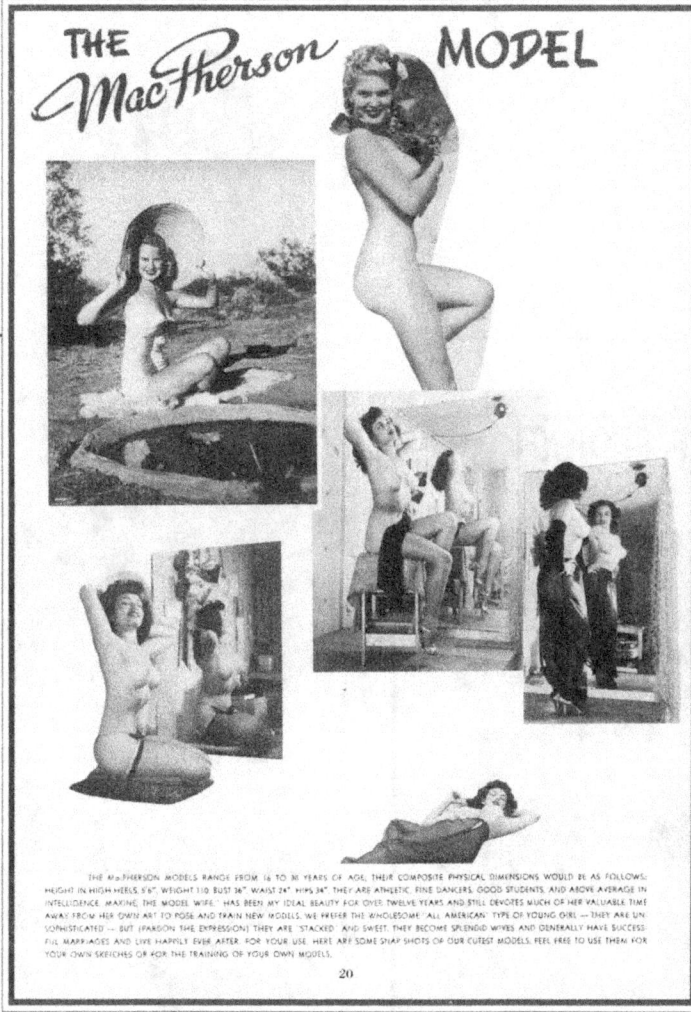

A page from "Pin-up Art," which sold 100,000 copies.

But eventually, they were able to move into their dream home, which they had named "Cliffhaven." It was featured in Sunset Magazine and written up in all the local papers, becoming well-known, as was the artist-owner.

Walter Foster published a book for Earl called *Pin-Up-Art*, with Annette on the cover. It sold one-hundred thousand copies in the United States and abroad. Meanwhile, Shaw-Barton was circulating Earl's art all over the Western Hemisphere.

Earl MacPherson hired an apprentice, Jerry Thompson, whom he says was "an ambitious and good artist." Earl built a second small studio under the cliff for his new assistant. Together, they almost doubled the art production. One day, the two of them were working in the small studio, which was heated by a small woodburning stove, when Earl became overheated. He stepped outside into a cold, damp fog rolling in off the Pacific and got a chill. By the next day, Earl had a raging fever and was taken to the hospital by ambulance. The diagnosis was polio! He spent the next two months in the San Diego County Hospital. Finally. he was sent home in a wheelchair, with a former navy nurse to assist him. Earl says:

"I was far from well; my legs felt useless. But we turned the studio into a small hospital and I directed Jerry's art production from my wheelchair. Then the doctor stopped by and insisted that I needed a drier climate. He sent me inland to a friend's cottage at Warner's Springs. There was a big, hot swimming pool out back in which I could exercise.

"It worked! By the next summer, I was able to walk with a cane. I had worked out a method with Jerry, whereby I would give him the sketch ideas, he would pick them up and go back to Del Mar to do the working sketches, and then bring them back to me for the finishing touches. Now Jerry started taking us back to "Cliffhaven" for the weekends, but everytime the fog rolled in from the ocean, the pain in my legs was unbearable.

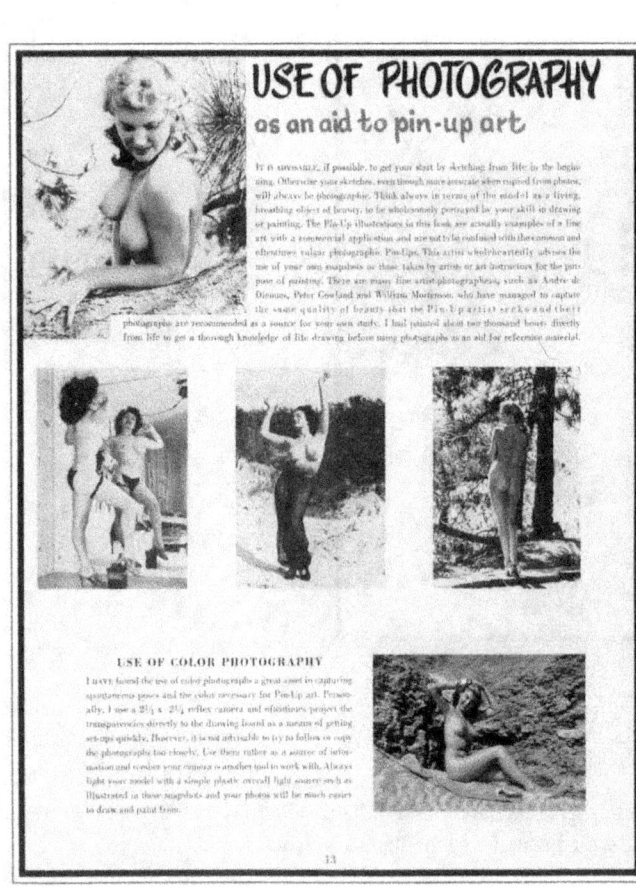

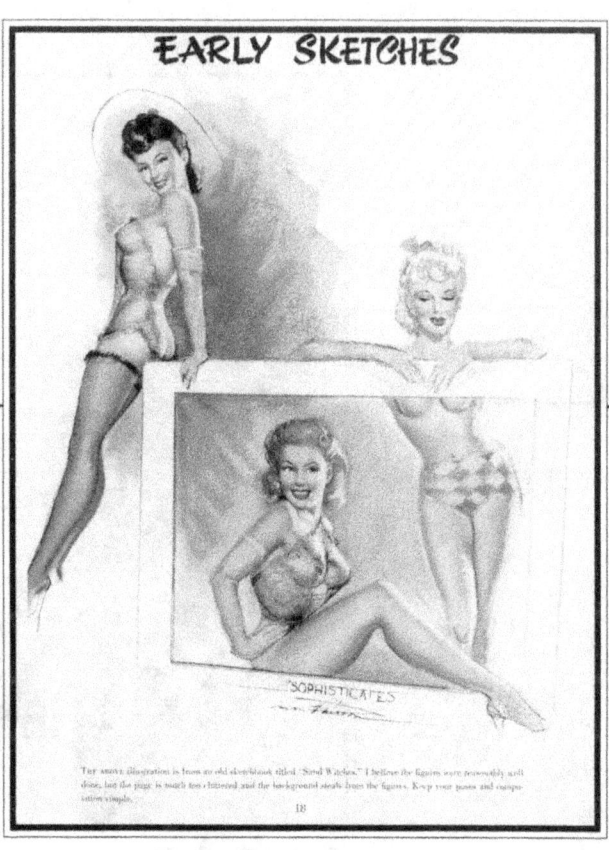

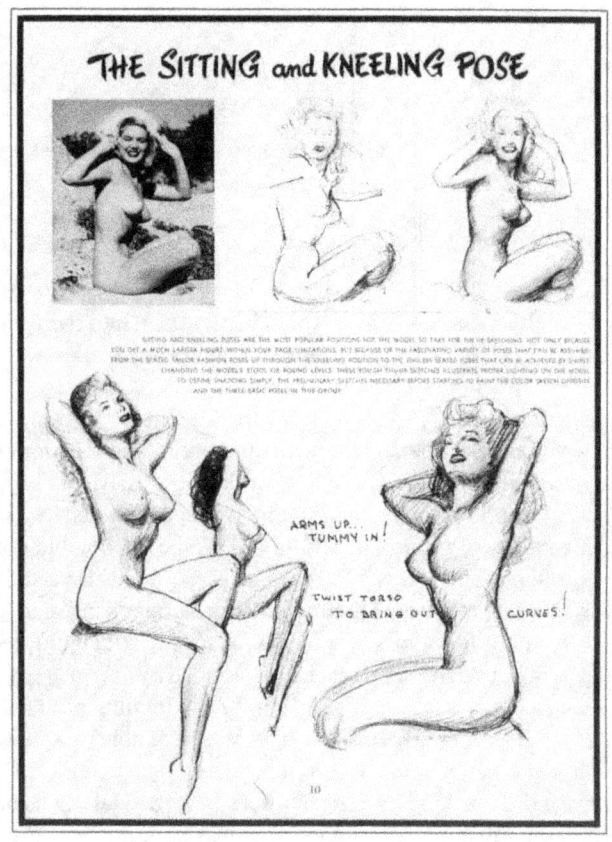

Pages from my book ,"Photographic Art."

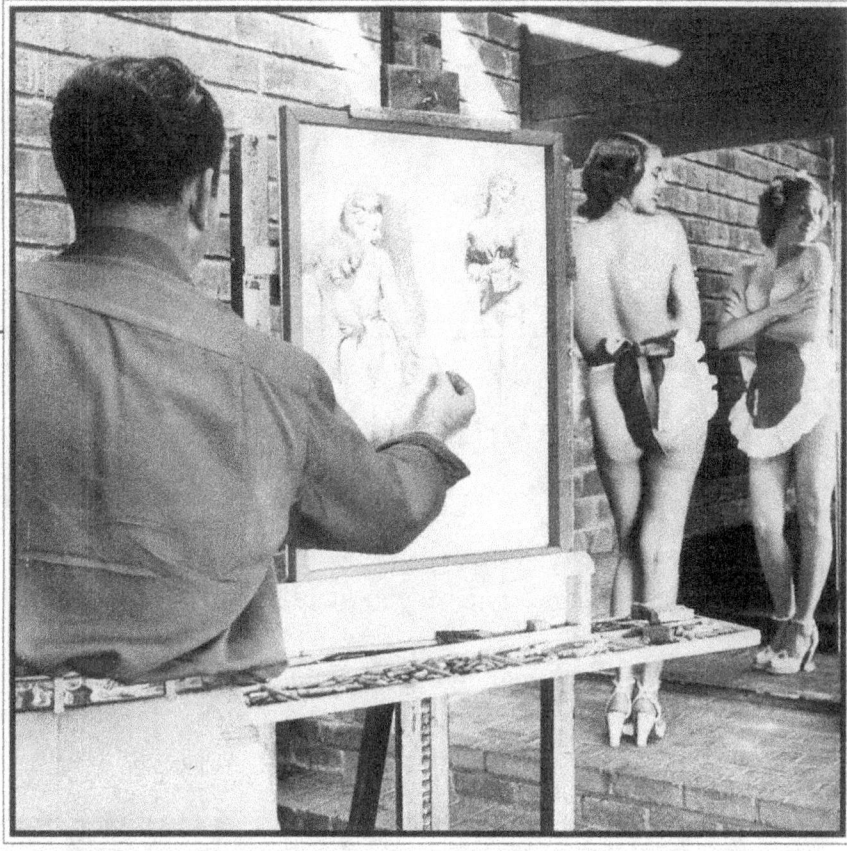

Posed photo at "Cliffhaven," for "Popular Photography" magazine.

Reluctantly, Earl and Annette decided to sell "Cliffhaven" and move to Phoenix, Arizona, with its dry climate.

It was in Phoenix, after Earl, Annette and Brian had settled in, that Earl was informed by the representative from Shaw-Barton that sales were slipping. However, Earl kept busy. By now, he was emceeing a television show for the Arizona Home Builders and considering building another dream home for Annette.

Dropped by the Home Builders, when they discovered that Earl was more interested in custom homes than mass produced ones, he went over to a rival network and started the "Mac Pherson Home Show." This time he was sponsored by the Department of Architecture in Arizona State College at Tempe. Under their auspices, Earl sponsored a contest for student architects, resulting in plans for his new home, "Casa Futura."

Life seemed good again. They had a new home. Brian was in private school. The television show went off the air when their home was finished, but Earl expected to be occupied again with his art career.

Earl relates what happened next:

Oliver Stevning flew out from Shaw-Barton, unexpectedly, in the spring.

"'Earl, I've bad news for you," he said.

"'Sales haven't picked up?' I asked.

"'Worse than that. They're dead," Stevning responded.

"I was forty-six years old and at the top of my profession. Except suddenly I had no profession. Coupled with the fact that television advertising was beginning to ruin the calendar business was the startling discovery that once again my art career was being ruined by photography."

Earl continues his explanation:

"After World War II, under the G. I. Bill, thousands of ex-G. I.'s had studied photography. All at once, the advertising and publication market was flooded with good nude photos, helping to launch the Playboy–type magazine. Art directors could now buy a nude photo for fifty dollars, whereas they had been paying at least one thousand dollars for a pastel pin-up from an artist such as myself. My comfortable five-figure income went to nothing in ninety days."

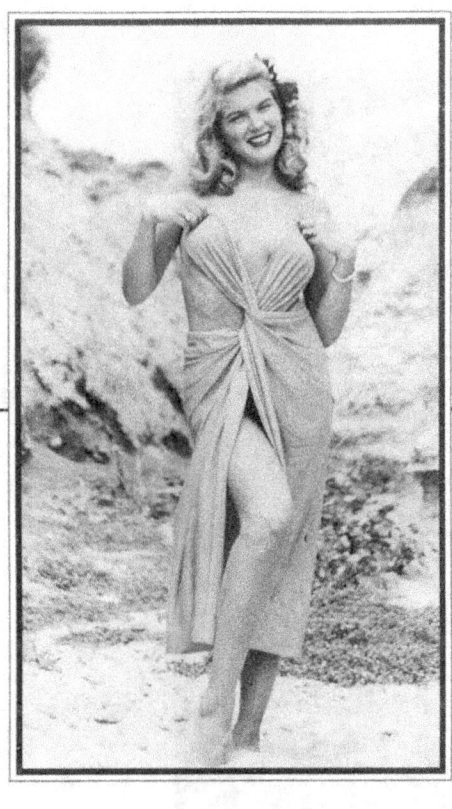

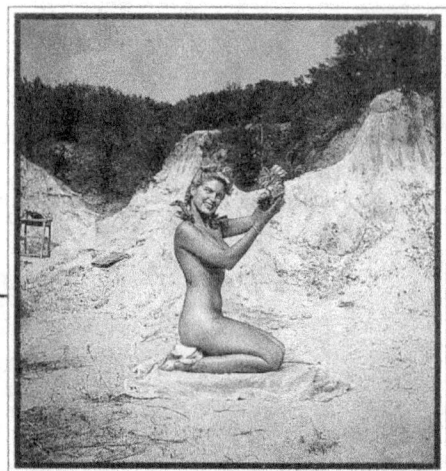

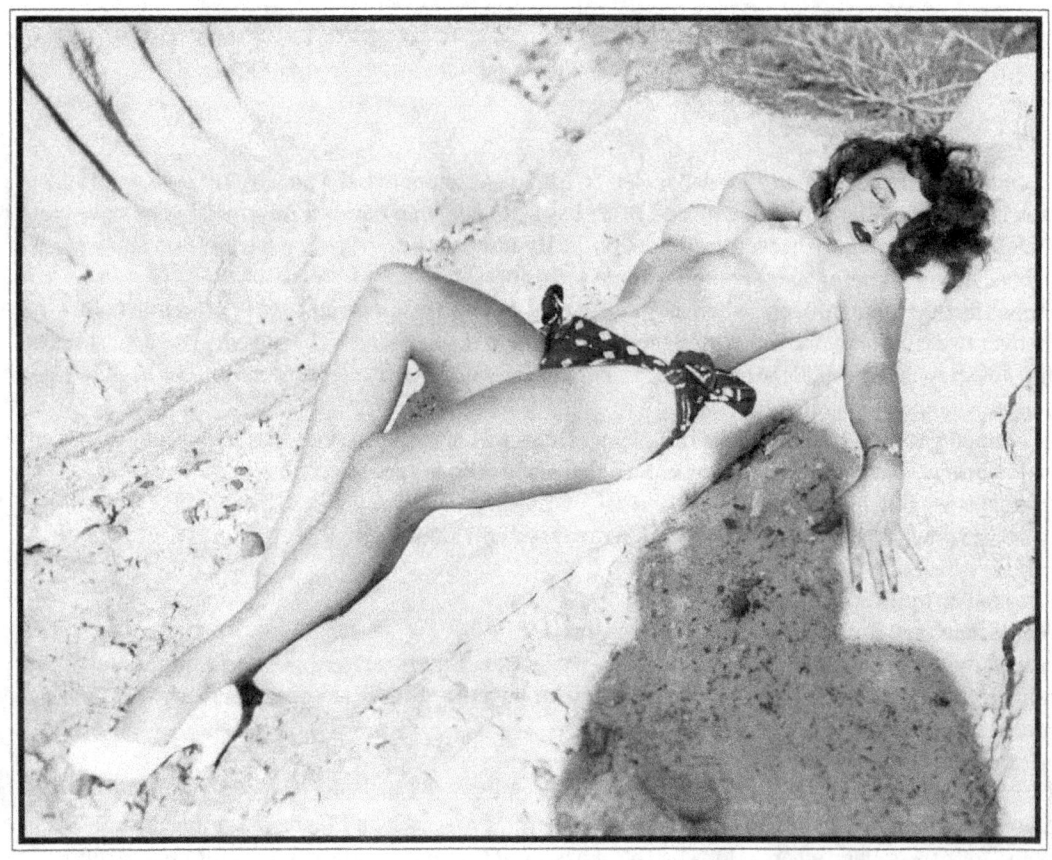

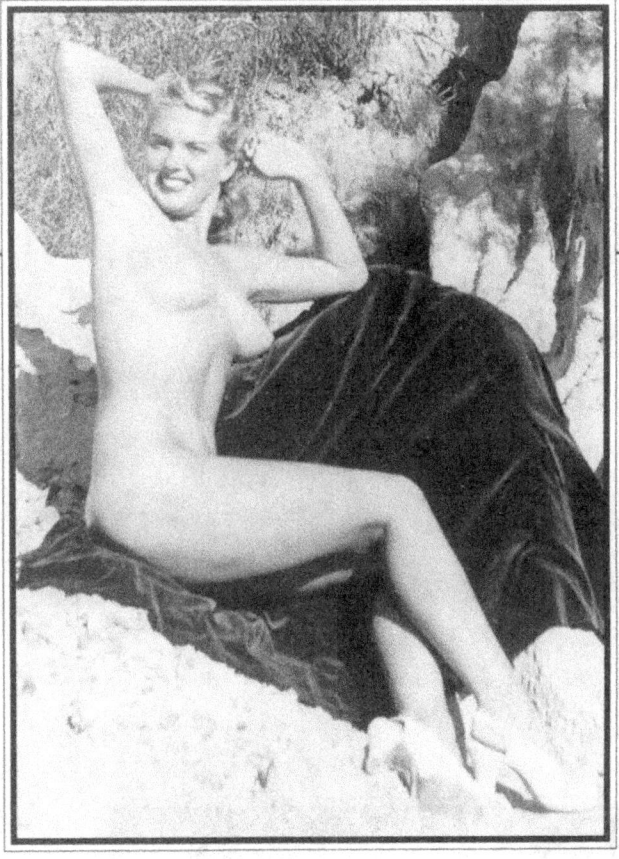

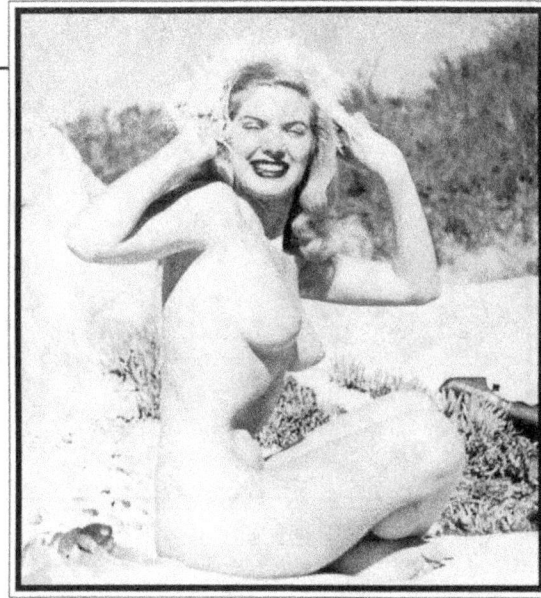

Uprooting his family again, Earl sold Annette's second dreamhouse, and the family elected to move to Tahiti and travel in the South Pacific. They stayed in Tahiti only a short time, after learning that Earl's old friend Del had gone to live in France. Moving to New Zealand for a while, they eventually settled on the Hawaiian island of Kauai, and operated the Polynesian Inn and Resort. Earl continued painting, doing Polynesians on a black velvet background.

After one horrendous hurricaine, Annette insisted that thay return to Arizona as soon as possible. Earl agreed because he was interested in trying to find out if there was oil on the Oklahoma property that "Old Bill" had left to him and his mom when he died.

When the oil well failed, after Earl had sunk all his available money into it, Annette left him for a wealthy Arizona businessman. Earl was devastated. He spent the next few years working at various jobs and travelling. Always, he kept up his painting and artwork.

More recently, Earl has returned to Prescott, Arizona, to paint Western Art. He married one of Prescott's most desirable widows, Reathel Gammill Jackson, the founding president of the Prescott Fine Arts.

Earl says,"Meeting Reathel has been the most rewarding and leveling influence in my life. It came about as a direct result of my most inspiring project, that of painting portraits of Jesus of Nazareth on Arizona flagstone.

"These 'Christones' are now cemented into the entryways and prayer chapels of several of Arizona's finest churches where they will endure and guarantee this artist a measure of immortality."

Earl MacPherson sums up his career with these remarks:

"Ideally, an artist's life is worth the struggle: especially if along the way he has not only learned how to make money with his art, but also how to have fun and see something of this glorious world while doing it."

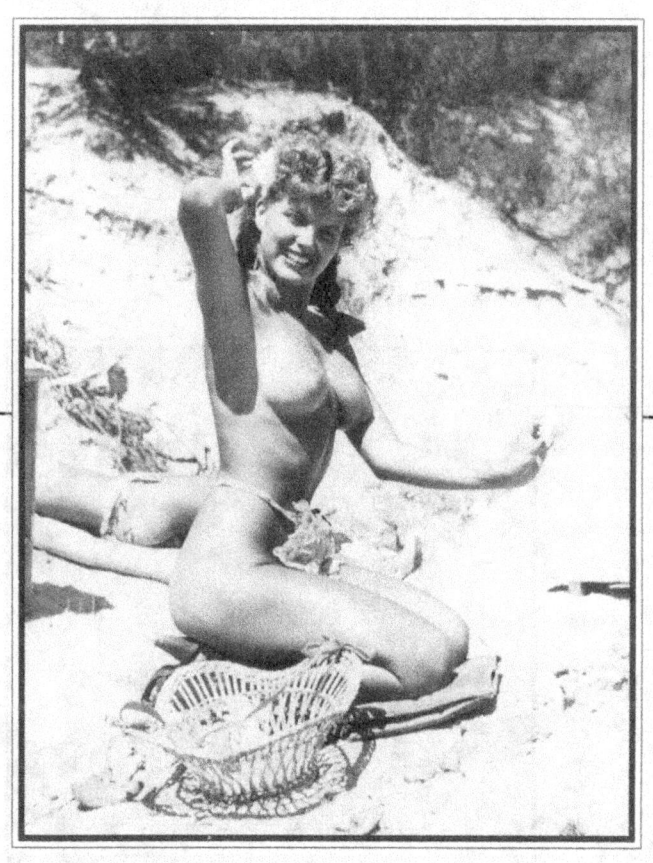

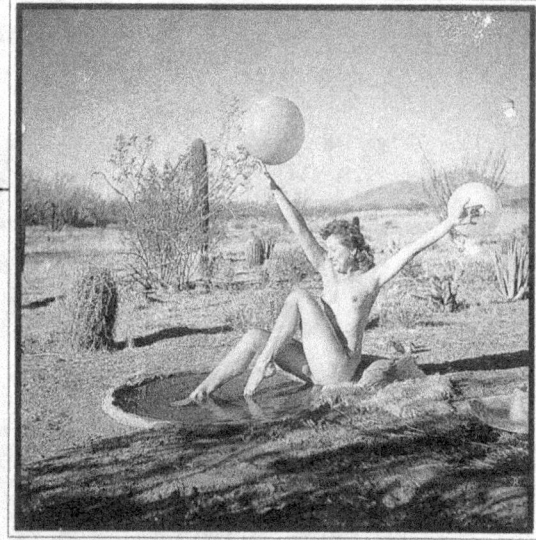

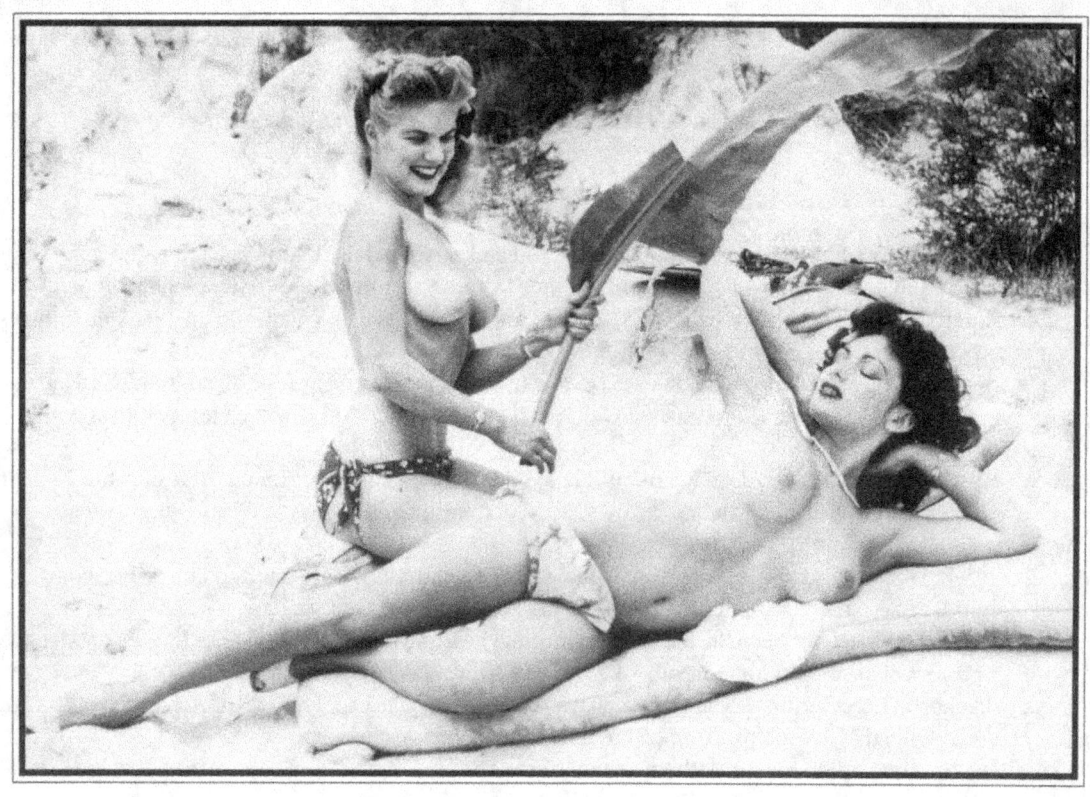

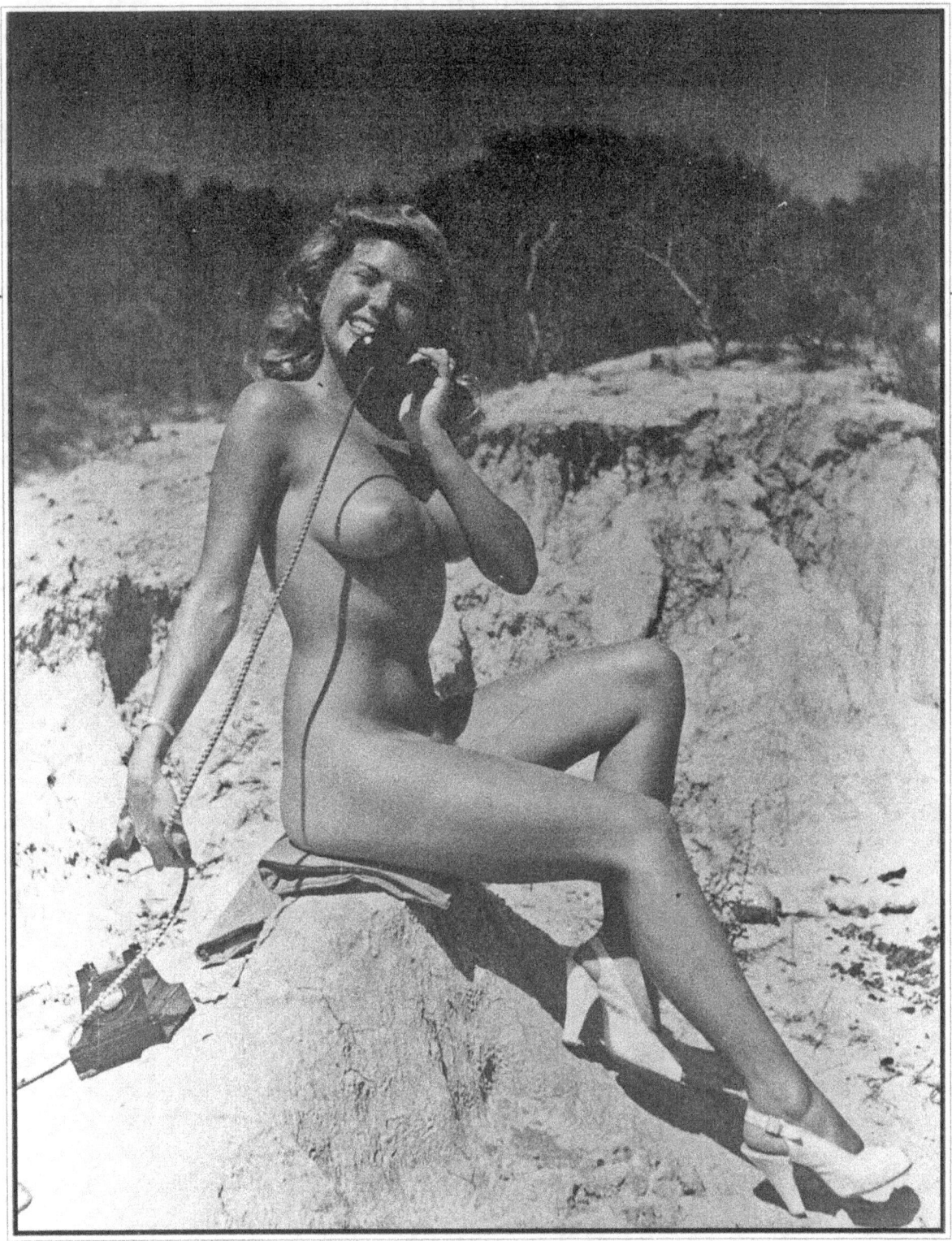

"Adios to my favorite models and the glamour they inspired me to capture with pastels and camera!"

mac Pherson

Addendum
in this Binary Publications' editon (2014)
compared to the 1991 Stubur Edition.

Earl MacPherson died in December 1993, less than two years after releasing
the original edition of this book.

We are proud to be able to bring it back and offer new audiences a
chance to see just a small amount of Earl's artwork and get some insights
into his incredible life.

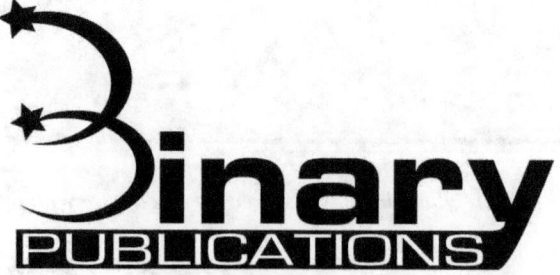

www.binarypublications.com

www.ingramcontent.com/pod-product-compliance
Lightning Source LLC
Chambersburg PA
CBHW080848170526
45158CB00009B/2674